WHOLENESS

WHOLENESS

ON EDUCATION, BUCKMINSTER FULLER, AND TAO

ALEX GERBER JR.

Gerber Educational Resources
Kirkland, Washington

. ACKNOWLEDGMENTS

My deepest appreciation to mentors, colleagues, and friends who, directly and indi-rectly, contributed to this book—Anne Spellicy, Joan Daly, Merrill Ring, Elfleda Tate, William F. O'Neill, David V. Tiedeman, Anne Miller-Tiedeman, Francis Klein, Carol Lynch, Rocky Stump, William Stump, Lorri Busse, Joel Porter Munsey, Don C. Maier, Daniel Larner, Larrene Shannon, Harold Nelson, Linda Lyman, Ardis O'Hara, Art Pozner, David Dufty, Melanie Marx, Sheila Kenny, Whitney Alexander, Alexis Traynor-Kaplan, Richard Kaplan, Joan Waiss, Chery Pinton, Max Pinton, Nick Consoletti, Martin Bozlee, Diane Adair, Martha Austin, Holly Crownhart, Amy Brightman, Alesa Lightbourne, Scott Van Verst, J. Baldwin, Bonnie and Tony DeVarco, Glen Velez, David Brunn, Bob Quinn, Cindy Matthews, Shelley Sapyta, Molly Murrah, Paul Langland, and Sally Polk and the staff of the Kirkland, Washington, branch of the King County Library System.

To those connected with the Buckminster Fuller Institute—Allegra Fuller Snyder, Jaime Snyder, John Ferry, Lauren Darges, Deborah Grace, Janet Brown, Jackie Lohrke, and Gary Milliken.

To Tamara Belland, Richard von Kleinsmid, John Thompson, and Ruth Thompson.

To Lonnie Maxfield, Jivan Institute, Bellevue, Washington.

To Ron Miller, Foundation for Educational Renewal, Brandon, Vermont.

To my loving sisters and their families.

Dedicated to my parents
in love and gratitude.

Wholeness: On Education, Buckminster Fuller, and Tao
Published by Gerber Educational Resources
Post Office Box 2997, Kirkland, Washington 98083, USA
(To order publications: www.wholenessbook.com)

Library of Congress Control Number: 00-132288
ISBN 0-9635367-1-0

Credits for previously published material appear on page 4.

Printed in the United States of America on recycled paper.

1 3 5 7 9 10 8 6 4 2

Contents

WHOLENESS

Let the beauty we love be what we do.

RUMI

INTRODUCTION

Awakening to wholeness may be the single most important event in anyone's life. This fundamental evolution refers to experiencing and valuing the interconnectedness of creation, the oneness of being. The whole, which encompasses all subjects, experiences, and perceptions, is the arena in which *everything* occurs, the essential point of reference. This book examines the whole as a "subject" in its own right, focusing on its components, significance, and practical applications. Of course wholeness is really not a subject at all; it is a state of being, an experience, a perspective—although wholeness transcends description.

Much has already been said about wholeness, holistic education, and the need for humans to accord with the rest of nature, but many people are still unfamiliar with these vital concepts and how they relate to our present and future options. Still others value the idea of wholeness but don't yet apply its wisdom in their daily lives.

Awakening to wholeness implies an ongoing process. One might ask, if someone can conceptualize wholeness, isn't the consciousness already present? The apparent contradiction of endeavoring to become whole, which the sages say we already are, is a familiar theme on the path of personal discovery. Even though wholeness is inherent, this doesn't mean we are aware of it, or rather, that we have remembered it.

People from all cultures and times have reiterated the truth that each human's birthright is to experience wholeness, a message that has particular significance at this time. As society comes to recognize how many problems and how much misery is associated with fragmentation and disconnection, wholeness will be seen as the only antidote.

Although omnipresent, the whole can seem elusive, vanishing like a bubble when dissected. This book presents one attempt to trace the untraceable.

NOTE TO READERS

Extensive reference notes are included for those who are interested; those who are not can happily ignore them. There are several reasons for this style of presentation. Because the idea of wholeness has endured from time immemorial, any nonfiction book that engages and examines it will to some extent be a synthesis of existing information. Also, this style presents the material directly, without interjecting my personal story. Finally, references provide easy avenues for further exploration; though relevant to people in all walks of life, this book may be particularly useful for study in such fields as education, philosophy, whole systems, and international relations.

CHAPTER 1

Education

The most important fact about Spaceship Earth:
An instruction book didn't come with it.

R. BUCKMINSTER FULLER

Context: A World Blind to the Whole

In these complex times, many people feel an increasing hunger for personal and planetary transformation. Although some of the environmental, social, and psychological factors wreaking havoc in the world have always been present, humans are now at a turning point. The quality of our collective future on this planet depends upon people becoming conscious of the whole and connecting with it.

Dictionaries define *whole* as "entire . . . total . . . complete . . . undivided." Wholeness may appear too abstract or impractical to study as a subject in its own right. Because the totality exceeds any words used to define it, an examination of the concept will require some intuition. In this book, the term "education" is used in its broadest sense, encompassing the ongoing process of learning and experiencing in every domain of life.

There are many possible ways to approach wholeness—through the avenues of philosophy, education, health, history, design, spirituality, and the environment, to name a few. Any subject can serve as an entrance point, but since the environment sustains every form of life on Earth, it is useful to begin here.

This book explores options for a brighter future. First, however, it is necessary to examine what is happening in the world around us.

While the following facts may seem harsh, a clear understanding of the situation is essential if we are to improve it.

If this is an ordinary day on planet Earth, 17 million tons of carbon will be added to the atmosphere as a result of fossil fuel burning, 169 square miles of forest (net) will be converted to other uses, 42 square miles of agriculturally useful drylands will become desert, more than 74 species will vanish in the rain forests alone, more than three million tons of topsoil will be lost to water erosion in just the United States (not including losses from wind erosion), 435 tons of chloro-fluorocarbons (CFCs) will be produced worldwide, and the human population will increase by 210,000. Within a year, more than six billion tons of carbon will be added to the atmosphere as a result of fossil fuel burning; an area of forest greater than the size of Florida will be gone; more than 27,000 species will become extinct in the rain forests alone; and Earth's population will have increased by 77 million.[1]

Synthetic airborne chemicals are drastically altering the atmosphere. The worldwide increase in skin cancer is directly linked to the reduction of the stratospheric ozone layer that protects against excessive ultraviolet radiation (UV).[2] Although it took millions of years to create this natural planetary sunscreen, the ozone layer has been radically depleted in a few decades. In addition to the antarctic ozone hole first observed in the mid-1980s, scientists have found similar problems in both temperate and arctic regions.[3]

The Union of Concerned Scientists points out that the atmospheric concentration of carbon dioxide (in part, a by-product of fossil fuel use implicated in global warming) is "already nearly 30 percent higher today than it was before the Industrial Revolution, and it continues to rise."[4] While ozone depletion and rising levels of greenhouse gases are often presented as separate phenomena, a feedback loop does exist between them.[5]

Another critical environmental issue is deforestation. In addition to ruining something of beauty, with intrinsic value, deforestation leads to topsoil erosion, water pollution, flooding, and species extinction. Since forests are crucial for cloud building, their depletion creates droughts and contributes to global warming.[6] Tropical rain forests are particularly vulnerable and, although they account for only 7 percent of the world's total land mass, more than 50 percent of the species of organisms in the world live there. At the present rate of deforestation, half of the remaining rain forests, along with one-tenth to one-quarter of the rain-forest species, will be gone by 2022.[7]

"Biological diversity is the key to the maintenance of the world as we know it," notes the Harvard biologist Edward O. Wilson.[8] Yet, according to the United Nations Environmental Program, vertebrate and vascular plant species alone are disappearing at fifty to one hundred times the "expected background" rate,[9] an effect attributed for the most part to current commercial logging, farming, and fishing practices.[10] Wilson states that "humanity has initiated the sixth great extinction spasm, rushing to eternity a large fraction of our fellow species in a single generation."[11] He has described the situation as "humanity versus the natural world."[12]

As only one example of the consequences of biodiversity loss, consider the worldwide importance of plant-based medicines. Billions of people rely on wild plants as sources of healing agents (as whole plants, parts of plants, and in the form of crude extracts), and more than 25 percent of all prescription drugs in the United States are derived from such plants (another 13 percent come from micro-organisms and 3 percent from animals—for a total of more than 40 percent that are derived from various organisms).[13] Unknown numbers of species that might have become sources of medicines are being wiped out before they can be investigated or even discovered.

Millions of tons of synthetic chemical compounds are released into the environment annually.[14] In the United States, of the 3,000 chemicals that are most widely used, fewer than 7 percent have a full set of baseline testing data, and 43 percent have no data whatsoever.[15] Organophosphates, a type of insecticide commonly used in the U.S., have been found to be neurotoxic and hormone-disrupting to children.[16] Men living in the U.S. now have a lifetime risk of one in two for developing cancer; for women the probability is one in three.[17]

Plutonium, the most dangerous and long-lived of the radioactive by-products, remains poisonous to some degree for hundreds of thousands of years. Containers have not been devised that can last for such an enormous time span, and quantities of this element have been released into the environment, both accidentally and intentionally.[18]

Destruction of the ecosystem leads to the destruction of human life. In 1993, the Union of Concerned Scientists issued their "World Scientists' Warning to Humanity":

> Human beings and the natural world are on a collision course. . . . If not checked, many of our current practices . . . may so alter the living world that it will be unable to sustain life in the manner that we know. Fundamental changes are urgent if we are to avoid the collision our present course will bring about. . . .
>
> Our massive tampering with the world's interdependent web of life—coupled with the environmental damage inflicted by deforestation, species loss, and climate change—could trigger widespread adverse effects, including unpredictable collapses of critical biological systems whose interactions and dynamics we only imperfectly understand. . . .
>
> No more than one or a few decades remain before the chance to avert the threats we now confront will be lost and the prospects for humanity immeasurably diminished. . . .
>
> [We] senior members of the world's scientific community . . . hereby warn all humanity of what lies ahead. A great change in our stewardship of the earth and the life on it is required, if vast human misery is to be avoided and our global home on this planet is not to be irretrievably mutilated.[19]

A similar warning was given by the French explorer, inventor, and environmentalist Jacques Cousteau (1910-1997), who, according to an Associated Press article, in his final book summarized our current course in these terms:

The road to the future leads us smack into the wall. We simply rico-
chet off the alternatives that destiny offers: a demographic explosion
that triggers social chaos and spreads death, nuclear delirium and the
quasi-annihilation of the species. Our survival is no more than a question of 25, 50 or perhaps 100 years.[20]

Test-tube Earth

Some people believe that the severity of the environmental situation
is being blown out of proportion. "There is no real crisis," they
say. "Humans still exist despite decades of doomsday pronouncements"—a reversal on the fable of Chicken Little, who insisted "The
sky is falling!" when the disaster was only a falling acorn. The sky is
intact, but the protective ozone layer is deteriorating.

Numerous experts have warned about accelerated global
warming. Yet many U.S. energy companies and politicians from oil-
and coal-producing states continue to assert that there is uncertainty
about this phenomenon.[21] However, the United Nations Intergovernmental Panel on Climate Change, composed of more than 2,000
leading climatological scientists from more than 100 nations, reports
that "the balance of evidence suggests a discernible human influence
on global climate," that "greenhouse gas concentrations have continued to increase," and that more extreme climate events are to be
expected.[22] Although climates have shifted cyclically throughout
history, it is the current rate of change that is so disturbing.

While signals of global warming are becoming more prevalent,
some researchers point to climatic manifestations that are usually
precursors of an ice age. Perhaps the two conditions are not mutually exclusive. Whatever the case, it is certainly foolish to take
chances with our life-supporting atmosphere, a system we know so
little about. No one can predict the point of instability at which a
momentous shift may occur because of an overload of carbon dioxide,

chlorine in various forms (implicated in the thinning of the ozone layer),[23] or other chemicals such as methyl bromide—all of which are being released into the atmosphere by humans. This scenario could be compared to the critical point in a titration procedure at which one additional drop of a chemical suddenly shifts the *nature* of the compound to which it is added. While this comparison may seem to present problems of scale, the same type of precipitous change could well occur in Earth's atmosphere.[24]

Even if atmospheric alterations were suddenly to cease, momentum must still be considered. Imagine a fully loaded supertanker that has been directed to stop—it still travels five miles before coming to a halt. The Union of Concerned Scientists notes that if most ozone-depleting chemicals were phased out immediately, "the damage to the ozone layer will continue to increase for decades, and may persist for a century or more, because of substances already emitted that have not yet risen to an altitude where they can do damage."[25]

Most people still do not sense the impact of cumulative ecosystem destruction, evidenced by the fact that remedial action is given such low priority. This demonstrates how disconnected from the whole the populace has become.

It is argued that if we try to save as many of the endangered fishes, bugs, and birds as possible, the economy will suffer. There is much evidence to show this would not be the case,[26] but calibrating environmental protection to economic performance misses the point. According to Paul and Anne Ehrlich of Stanford University's Center for Conservation Biology,

> A politician who says something like "The time has come to put the economy ahead of the environment" clearly doesn't understand that the economy is a wholly owned subsidiary of natural ecosystems and that the natural environment supplies humanity with an indispensable array of goods and services. He or she undoubtedly also does not understand key threats to those ecosystems such as population growth and rapid climate change.[27]

The Ehrlichs also note,

> A lack of understanding about matters fundamental to our existence highlights not only a failure of our educational system but also the failure of professional ecologists to communicate their knowledge to the general public.[28]

While the world's news media are presumably responsible for relaying vital information to the public, most of them have come to be controlled by transnational corporations,[29] a situation that can lead to conflicts of interest. For example, companies whose environmental practices should be exposed may be providing the media with significant advertising revenues or may themselves be divisions of the media's parent companies. Thus it is little wonder that vast numbers of people have received inadequate or erroneous information about the environmental crisis (and other issues).[30]

Common sense dictates that we heed the warnings of scientists rather than the platitudes of politicians, nonindependent researchers, and those with special interests who try to convince us that "everything is just fine." We cannot afford to assume that the Union of Concerned Scientists and the Intergovernmental Panel on Climate Change are wrong. Some people are convinced that our environmental crisis is merely part of the ebb and flow in a series of normal occurrences, or that these are signs of the "end time" prophesied in the Bible. Others justify inaction by preferring "nonintervention in the natural course of things," the Taoist concept of *wu-wei*.[31] Cleaning up and protecting the environment, however, is no less natural than despoiling it, and the *wu-wei* attitude does imply spontaneous action appropriate to a given situation.[32]

Those who would minimize the environmental situation are encouraged to read *The Heat Is On: The High Stakes Battle over Earth's Threatened Climate,* by the Pulitzer Prize-winning journalist Ross Gelbspan; *Betrayal of Science and Reason: How Anti-Environmental Rhetoric Threatens Our Future,* by Paul and Anne Ehrlich; and the revised edition of *Nuclear Madness: What You Can Do,* by Helen Caldicott, M.D. (see appendix B).

The purpose of this discussion of the environment has been to establish a context for considering holistic principles. Ultimately, only personal inquiry will convince people of the ongoing and vastly underreported disabling of environmental systems.[33] This book is oriented to those who are coming into holistic awareness and who seek practical ways to improve the quality of life, not only for themselves but for others. As will become apparent, only through the holistic perspective can we accurately perceive the interconnectedness of our environmental, social, economic, governmental, and ethical predicament (see appendix E).

Our Predicament

Considering the timespan of human evolution and the vast potential of humankind—as evidenced by great genius and leadership, inventions and discoveries, works of art and literature—it is lamentable that the economic and political systems of "advanced" cultures are still based on the unenlightened rationales that "more is better" and "might makes right." In the name of "survival of the fittest" and ensuring "vital interests," our economic system creates an ever-widening gap between rich and poor as it dismantles the environment upon which we all depend. Even "lower" animals generally do not foul their own nests.

We would like to believe that the economy could continue growing for eternity with no ruinous environmental, social, and personal consequences. In Western culture and increasingly around the world, accumulating wealth is often the main pursuit in life. "Expand the economy" has become a mantra. When all measures of value, success, security, and progress are reduced to financial considerations, the environment and the human condition are neglected. The Union of Concerned Scientists states,

> Across the world, one person in five lives in absolute poverty, . . .
> one in ten suffers serious malnutrition; . . . more money is spent on
> weapons and armies than on health and education; . . . more money
> is flowing out of some of the poorest countries than is coming in—
> and one can see a global disaster in the making.[34]

Owing to the cumulative by-products of the prevailing system, the continued viability of the human species is now in question. While the media sporadically report on efforts to "save the planet," it is really humans and other species that are endangered.[35] Unfortunately, many people are so unconscious of the whole that save-the-planet messages fail to register.

Should continual economic growth be the predominant model, the highest purpose of human civilization? Continual growth is one characteristic of cancer that eventually destroys the host. (As we shall see, other options exist, such as steady-state economics,[36] ecosystem restoration to the extent possible, and government committed to the well-being of all.)

An economic system is just a construct—one way to understand, order, and value life. Before investigating alternatives it is necessary to examine the phenomena of fragmentation and cognitive discord. Like atmospheric carbon dioxide and ultraviolet radiation, these have always been with us; now they, too, have risen to crisis proportions.

Fragmentation and Cognitive Discord

People are continually advised which way is best. *"This* is the way it should be!" "No, no, no! *Our* way is right!" "Things are meant to be *that* way." "Buy this brand." "Buy that brand." "If you don't listen to me you'll be sorry." From family members, friends, teachers, clergy, politicians, advertisers, economists, commentators, talk show hosts, editorial writers, columnists, political cartoonists, authors, entertainers, spin doctors, and professional motivators through conversation, television, radio, movies, billboards, newspapers, magazines, books, pamphlets, newsletters, professional journals, lectures, the Web, videos, audiotapes, comic books, junk mail, e-mail, advertisements inside public transit and out, meetings, and telephone solicitations—ideas and products are constantly being pushed onto us: more, more, more! ad infinitum. The overload is so great that the information becomes meaningless. "Fly to Maui," "Vote for Fred," and "Save the Planet" all blur together.

Contributing to this cognitive discord, headlines in the news media about a given topic often contradict each other from day to day and sometimes within a single issue: Economic forecast bleak; economy rebounds! Rival factions clash; rival factions unite! As long as we receive our daily, mind-numbing infusion of "+ and -," it hardly seems to matter what the stories are, since they are soon forgotten anyway. Such dichotomies appear in the form of news breaks, "infotainment," expert commentary, ads, sermons, theories, hype, slogans, obfuscating imagery, confusional politics, mega-events, and grand public spectacles; and along with the unceasing noise of machines, the roar of traffic, mounting pressures of every kind—people often become fragmented. For many, there exists no time or sense of space to pull off the road and collect themselves, to pause and consider, or simply to rest for a moment. To be.

Through manipulation of information, economies, and events (as well as other factors), the discord as modeled above is continually augmented and reinforced.[37] In many homes, offices, schools, organizations, and places of worship, little or no encouragement is given to investigating options for our personal and collective well-being—or even to learning that they exist.

Much of the fragmentation within society is manifested in conditions that seem to be completely out of control: the environmental situation, racism, political corruption, and the threats of nuclear power, for example. Although many people remain hopeful, vast numbers seem to have abandoned all expectations. Despondent, lonely, confused, alienated, stressed, embittered, angry, isolated, or otherwise adrift in life, they can't conceive of enlightened understanding, authenticity, wise guidance, or peace of mind.

Some believe that fragmentation and cognitive discord are unalterable aspects of human nature. But these widespread phenomena are both a result, and a cause, of perceiving and acting from a perspective fixed only on "the parts."

Is There Another Way?

Multitudes of people yearn for a guiding light—a comforting, inspiring beacon they do not have to be harangued into following, live in fear of, or meet firsthand only after they die. The wise do not cultivate reverence for one particular religion, ethnic group, sect, or tribe at the expense of others. A genuine beacon would rise above the many differing belief systems and life patterns that divide us, inspiring compassion and connection.

Is there a world view, a way of perceiving and acting, that people from all backgrounds and geographical locations can support as authentic—one that can restore a sense of healing, optimism, and hope throughout the world?

The Union of Concerned Scientists states,

> A new ethic is required—a new attitude towards discharging our responsibility for caring for ourselves and for the earth. We must recognize the earth's limited capacity to provide for us. We must recognize its fragility. We must no longer allow it to be ravaged. This ethic must motivate a great movement, convincing reluctant leaders and reluctant governments and reluctant peoples themselves to effect the needed changes.[38]

How can this occur? Even the experts contradict one another about environmental, economic, and social issues. Since their differing views are generally backed by research, which "truths" are accurate? In order to help ensure humanity's future, a new awareness needs to be translated into effective worldwide action. But awareness of what?

Both observation and intuition reveal that people may all too slowly be coming to realize they are part of an inseparable whole, a world community. While there is a burgeoning interest in the personal growth "movement"—evidenced, in part, by the growing number of self-help, self-awareness, and holistic healthcare programs as well as the explosion of publications on self-improvement and spirituality[39]—the world still awaits a collective shift of consciousness.

Which "Education"?

Scientists and others warn that fundamental changes are urgently needed, but what should those changes be, and which ones should come first? A transformation of consciousness is indicated, but according to whose blueprint? Since millions of people know better, why do assaults on Earth's life-support systems continue?

These questions present a major challenge pertaining to education. As we move into the twenty-first century, what kind of world do we really want? What options are available? How should we be educating ourselves and our children? What unifying ethic could benefit all life on the planet?

Among all the facts and "best advice" about how to live and think, is there a way that we can determine *for ourselves* viable answers to these questions? Is there some specific knowledge that can help us discern *for ourselves* which information is accurate? Given the pandemic disruptive effects of fragmentation and cognitive discord, how can we become balanced and fulfilled in our lives?

To answer these questions and to evaluate the many available "truths," a high level of discernment is required. A straightforward philosophical and educational process does exist that can help people become more effective with this faculty.

To Be Optimally Effective

R. Buckminster Fuller, whose contributions are examined in the next chapter, taught that an individual's relative effectiveness in any area is directly related to the ability to perceive and act comprehensively—"from the whole." Fuller stated, *"To be optimally effective, undertake at outset the most comprehensive task in the most comprehensive and incisively detailed manner."*[40]

If this statement is true, what makes it so? Several elements are involved: determining what it means to be optimally effective, determining what constitutes the most comprehensive task, and determining the most comprehensive and incisively detailed manner for accomplishing such a task.

Learning more about what Fuller termed "comprehensivity"—the "subject" of wholeness—is a logical first step in both identifying comprehensive tasks and learning comprehensive ways to undertake them.[41]

"Defining" Wholeness

As mentioned in the introduction, wholeness is not a subject in the usual sense and cannot be learned or defined. Still, there are things *about* it that can be learned. This central paradox appears throughout the book.

The term *wholeness* means the quality or state of being whole. "The whole" refers to *everything*—the entirety of creation, all that is, undivided, without diminution. *Whole* is the word from which *health, heal,* and *holy* are derived. *Holistic,* from the Greek *holos* (whole), refers to understanding reality in terms of integrated wholes whose properties cannot be reduced to smaller units.[42] It also pertains to the integral, functional relationship of the whole to the parts in any context or system (a tree, a body, an ecosystem, a household, a society, a planet).

In this book, the terms *wholeness, oneness,* and *comprehensivity* are used interchangeably to denote consciousness of the whole. Whereas a nonholistic approach "doesn't see the forest for the trees," a holistic approach perceives and values the forest—all forests. This strategy includes holistic action, not just words and theories. Wholeness also implies integrity, one definition of which is "the state of being whole, entire, or undiminished."[43]

Definitions of wholeness will always fall short, since language itself is only a part of the whole (just as words are only a part of communication, along with sighs, gestures, touch, facial expressions, pheromones, body language, and other signals). Likewise, it is impossible to fully understand wholeness because the realm of things understood is only part of all that is.

Although undefinable and enigmatic, the whole can be felt or intuited, and some of its attributes and manifestations can be observed. We can perceive its signs and messages, but we must still learn how to read them. This is the process of awakening to wholeness. As holistic realities are illuminated, this awareness can help each of us become "optimally effective" in environmental, educational, and all other endeavors, including the "comprehensive task" of discerning among the multitude of competing advice and belief systems.

Wholeness—the Fourth "R"

The three Rs (reading, writing, and arithmetic) have long been considered the pillars of education. Metaphorically speaking, wholeness is the fourth "R," a basic "subject" most of us were never exposed to, since most of our teachers and parents knew little about it. While the three Rs are learnable skills, wholeness refers to the totality. The "fourth R" metaphor merely signifies that wholeness, in addition to meaning "everything," is one of the fundamentals of education. Wholeness may really be the first "R" (if an actual R word is desired, use *relatedness*).

Holistic education is unfragmented *living* education that integrates all aspects of existence. Though holism may appear to be just one more "ism," it is different from other philosophies; it is a meta-philosophy, a philosophy of philosophy. Attempting to classify holism within existing schools of Western philosophic thought—idealism, realism, and pragmatism, for example—presents difficulty, but other models do fall under it since this philosophy pertains to the comprehensive nature of reality, the whole picture.

Although *holistic* may be an overused buzzword, it is still the best description for the relationship between the whole and its parts. Labeling it "new age" is inaccurate since the whole is timeless (concepts of time being part of the whole, not the other way around).

Most education, even the education of teachers, is designed to increase a person's "database" or store of knowledge. Accruing knowledge is necessary; however, the philosophical base, which ideally underpins our choices in life, should be given priority. Because there is simply too much information to store in one's head, education must show *how* to go about learning—not only how to find and use information, but also how to determine what is worthwhile to investigate in the first place, how to evaluate what one learns, and how to discover its connections to the whole.

The holistic approach to education is not primarily concerned with specific issues, ideologies, statistics, or historical debates. Instead, it provides the philosophical base necessary for answering the "big questions" in life posed above: What kind of world do we want? What options are available? How should we be educating ourselves and our children? What unifying ethic could benefit all life on the planet?

According to the educator and author Ron Miller, holistic education addresses "the fragmentation, alienation, competition, violence, and gross materialism that pervade much of life . . . seek[ing] to heal the many divisions our civilization has induced between mind and body, intellect and emotion, rationality and intuition, science and art, individual and community, humanity and the natural world." Such education emphasizes "the ultimate unity, relatedness, and inherent meaningfulness of all existence."[44]

Awakening to wholeness involves several aspects: the personal discovery of wholeness, the recognition of attributes of the whole, and the exploration of holistic strategies for education and for daily life. These aspects naturally overlap and intertwine.

In the same way that reading and writing require knowledge of words, spelling, and sentence structure, and arithmetic involves addition, multiplication, etc., wholeness has its own fundamentals.

Features of Holism

SYNERGY

A central feature of the whole is *synergy,* which Buckminster Fuller defined as "behavior of whole systems unpredicted by the behavior of the parts taken separately."[45] A popularized definition is "the whole is greater than the sum of its parts." Like gravity, magnetism, and radioactivity, synergy is an operational reality in the world.

One graphic example of synergy that Fuller used comes from the field of metallurgy. Individually, the elements iron, chromium, and nickel have certain characteristics. But when combined with carbon, manganese, and other minor constituents they become chrome-nickel-steel, an alloy much stronger and more durable than any of the original elements. Able to withstand extremely high temperatures, this alloy is used in the manufacture of jet engines (a development that has changed our perception of time and space).[46] Fuller explained,

> It is a very popular way of thinking to say that a chain is no stronger than its weakest link. That seems to be very logical to us. Therefore, we feel that we can predict things in terms of certain minor constituents of wholes. That is the way much of our thinking goes. If I were to say that a chain is as strong as the sum of the strengths of its links, you would say that is silly. If I were to say that a chain is

stronger than the sum of the strengths of all of its links, you might say that . . . is preposterous. Yet that is exactly what happens with chrome-nickel-steel. If our regular logic held true, then the iron as the weakest part ought to adulterate the whole: since it is the weakest link, the whole thing [should] break apart when the weakest link breaks down. . . .

[But] chrome-nickel-steel's weakest part does not adulterate the whole, . . . [so it doesn't dissolve] as does candy when the sugar dissolves.[47]

There are countless examples of the power of synergy. The impact and beauty of an entire orchestra playing a symphony is unpredicted by the same music played on individual instruments. For a visual example, consider the combined effect of colors in a rainbow. In the classroom, children directly experience synergy by working as a team (of course one can also experience synergy when working alone, if the approach is holistic).

The principle of synergy can be applied toward meeting basic human needs such as healthful food, affordable housing, and healthcare. By planning and acting from the holistic perspective, humanity could create an entirely new "alloy," a truly viable planetary civilization.

The chart in appendix E shows what happens when some of the inherently synergistic systems of Earth are caused to break down. Synergy can also manifest itself in ways that are detrimental to life, *adverse* net effects that are greater than the sum of the parts (as with lethal synergistic drug reactions). When people, corporations, and governments focus only on short-term gains, without regard to the whole, ultimately the well-being and survival of humanity are threatened.[48]

Given the massive momentum of environmental degradation as well as the many distressing social conditions in the world, policymakers and others in industry, government, and education would be wise to take full advantage of synergy—a powerful ally that can also benefit our personal lives. How can we take advantage of synergy? Just as one needs to be familiar with the principle of leverage in order to move heavy objects with a lever and fulcrum, a familiarity with the principle of synergy can help one become optimally effective in every endeavor.

Humans have greatly benefited from the focused use of forces such as gravity, magnetism, fire, and water. Gravity, for example, is a constant, yet it can be specifically employed to irrigate crops. Magnetism, always emanating from Earth's magnetic poles, becomes apparent through the needle of a compass. Similarly, synergy is an ever-present potential that can be purposefully focused by explicitly identifying and nurturing it in any domain of activity—by focusing *first* on the whole system, and then progressing to individual parts.

Why does this work? Nature functions as a whole, integrated, synergistic system. Synergy, by definition, is a phenomenon *of* the whole. *People can become optimally effective by aligning with the whole and its inherent synergy.* This alignment potentiates synergy, creating effects greater than the sum of individual actions. This is the reason that, in any domain of activity, it is optimally effective to undertake at the outset "the most comprehensive task" and to address all tasks comprehensively, as Buckminster Fuller advised. When one commences with the parts, which is the usual procedure, the infinitude of parts obscures the whole. Aligning with wholeness, however, may be easier said than done, because the whole can seem subtle, and many people lack the conceptual tools to relate in such broad terms—a situation this book is intended to help remedy.

When the whole is specifically identified as the arena—the true field of activity, the actual context—of our lives, vital interrelationships among the parts can then be discerned with greater clarity.

Since life functions as a whole, and education investigates life, education should be holistically oriented. One way teachers now apply the principle of synergy is by integrating the curriculum so that students develop multiple skills (in reading, spelling, math, history, geography, biology, creative writing, art) simultaneously through the study of a single topic such as potatoes, polar bears, or Tanzania.

Commencing with the whole and identifying synergistic connections will enhance any learning activity, whether in a first grade classroom or graduate seminar, a staff development program or wilderness retreat. Buckminster Fuller wrote,

> Synergy reveals a grand strategy of dealing with the whole instead of the tactics of our conventional educational system, which starts with parts and elements, adding them together locally without really understanding the whole.[49]

> The very integrity of our Universe is implicit in synergy.[50]

WHOLE-TO-PARTS ORIENTATION

Starting as it does with the parts, traditional Western education rarely, if ever, progresses to the whole. This approach is evident in most college catalogs, where knowledge is classified into minute specializations. Such compartmentalization is useful in some disciplines, but when it is the predominant approach, as in the physical sciences, social sciences, and teacher education programs, we fail to recognize the all-important reality of the whole. This omission has tragic consequences since life itself is a phenomenon of the whole.

Holism does not imply simplistically lumping everyone and everything together in one big "feel-good" mush. Nor does it require submerging oneself in some woozy, unthinking, vacuous "unity." Concern for the whole does not come at the expense of the parts since the parts are aspects of the whole; in fact they *are* the whole. Yet the whole is something more.

The whole-to-parts orientation is an *approach* to life and to education, a personal attitude rather than a closed, doctrinal system, a way of being as well as a way of doing. It reveals the "big picture" and at the same time works as a magnifying glass—a tool for discerning how to achieve optimal effectiveness and to enhance one's enjoyment of life. As individuals experience this nonquantifiable orientation, every encounter and activity is affected. Many educators have found that helping learners link their inner worlds with the unity of life is one of the most satisfying elements in education.

A crucial variable in determining whether students experience holistic connections is the teacher's own "holistic orientation." Paradoxically, proceeding from the whole to the parts both requires, and assists in developing, this orientation. From the outset, intuition is necessary for understanding and using these concepts.

Commencing with the whole and then moving to the particulars results in unfragmented education in which subjects and issues are investigated in relationship to the whole of life, the "field of activity" mentioned above. Many teachers already use an interdisciplinary approach; however, the main purpose of this book is to advance awareness of wholeness *itself* as a "subject." This is a key point. The next step is to provide courses in holistic theory and practice for teachers, followed by courses for their students—at all levels from preschool through graduate school. Such courses are also essential for administrators, parents, corporate and governmental policymakers, and everyone else.

Holistic education and the whole-to-parts orientation do not necessarily require overnight changes in lesson plans or infrastructure. Although holistic resources do exist,[51] once teachers embody a holistic attitude, all educational methods and experiences become suffused with it. Inherent connections to the whole are discovered. A certain milieu is created—indeed, this milieu is the totality, the whole, in which we all exist. As teachers learn more about this approach, ideas for holistic learning activities arise spontaneously; synergy is in play.

Even when teachers discover their own connections with the whole, some students may be so conditioned to a "parts" orientation that wholeness seems inconceivable. Fortunately, such perceptions can change. Introducing activities that focus on holistic interrelationships can revitalize learning as students become aware of the bigger picture. This awareness expands synergistically within students and teachers. Beyond awareness, a fundamental aspect of holistic education is its practical application in the world (discussed later in this chapter).

Learning to appreciate individuality and cultural diversity is another facet of holistic education. The notion of diversity, however, includes not only people and cultures, but all living creatures, all habitats (soils, rivers, oceans, etc.), the planet itself, and the universe. The ultimate diversity is the whole.

While academia generally emphasizes logical and quantitative analysis, holistic education requires an expanded viewpoint. Holistic education includes such analysis, but also values the process of perceiving and knowing intuitively. Therefore in this book, the terms "holistic approach," "living education," "whole-to-parts," "holistic orientation," and the "whole of life" are neither referenced nor defined objectively. One invariably discovers that words and explanations are inadequate when it comes to wholeness.

THE INVISIBLE REALM

The whole, by its nature, is greater than what can be experienced through the five senses. Although the totality is omnipresent, aspects of it are invisible. Thus, the invisible realm itself (a theme in Buckminster Fuller's work) is a vital aspect of holistic education.

Much of everyday reality exists in abstract and essentially invisible dimensions. For example, synergy, though very real, is intangible, like gravity or radioactivity. Only its effects are evident. Many factors that affect air, water, and food are imperceptible to all but the most sophisticated scientific instruments. Processes leading to such diseases as cancer or Alzheimer's often seem invisible because they occur so gradually. Chemical reactions that result in super-high-tech alloys are also generally unseen. Similarly, the phenomena of global warming and ozone depletion certainly exist, even though they are not easily perceived (and are therefore usually ignored).

Though most of the electromagnetic realm is invisible (except as registered through scientific instruments), it is integral to life. Healing, prayer, and love also exist in unseen realms that can only be felt or intuited.[52] Radio waves are constantly broadcast, but in order to hear music, one's radio must be turned on and tuned to the station. While the whole is ever present and accessible at any time, holistic education can help tune in the "station." Katya Walter writes in *Tao of Chaos,*

> The main difficulty with this holistic realm, of course, is that it flickers at the edge of awareness. It signals from beyond the fringe. It keeps fleeing from direct gaze. Thus it must be approached with the sidelong glance of holistic pattern recognition rather than the pinpoint glare of linear dissection.[53]

How can those who rely solely on tangible evidence come to accept nonquantifiable realities? By developing a holistic orientation—a softer focus, a mode of inquiry that is intuitive, interdisciplinary, cross-cultural. When circumstances warrant, objective rationales can be marshaled to support the holistic approach; however, holism incorporates and transcends such rationales by focusing on intuition as the all-important guide. To illustrate this point, consider that by the time we have scientifically proven the limits of Earth's life-support capabilities, those limits may already have been reached.

The "objective proof required" syndrome has a potentially fatal grip on humanity. But there is an antidote: embracing the lessons of wholeness and the invisible realm. In past centuries this knowledge was the domain of healers, philosophers, and mystics. Now that scientists are also demonstrating the reality of the invisible whole, the "objective proof required" syndrome may loosen its hold. Recognizing that invisible factors are vitally active in the universe is a major aspect of the paradigm shift now underway. Although numerous books and articles have examined this shift, because of its central importance a brief overview follows.

THE PARADIGM SHIFT

Paradigm is defined as "an example serving as a model; pattern."[54] The science historian and philosopher Thomas S. Kuhn (1922-1996), in his classic book *The Structure of Scientific Revolutions*, explained that the theoretical or conceptual models we hold as truths, and through which we perceive reality, are in actuality the latest in a series of paradigms that evolve gradually over the course of time.[55]

The shift in consciousness from Ptolemaic to Copernican astronomy provides one familiar example. The Greek mathematician, astronomer, and geographer Ptolemy (fl. 127-151 C.E.) perceived Earth as the fixed center of the universe, with other heavenly bodies moving around it. That paradigm faded away when the Polish astronomer Copernicus (1473-1543) demonstrated that Earth and other planets move around the sun.

As anomalies accumulate to the point where a predominant paradigm no longer accurately explains phenomena, and as a new theory becomes successful in doing so, a scientific revolution occurs. Kuhn observed that the imperatives and workings of paradigm shifts are not unique to the physical sciences. They apply to and in fact were borrowed from literature, the arts, political development, and other fields.[56]

As the systems theorist Fritjof Capra points out, humanity's social, political, economic, and environmental plights are all manifestations of a cultural crisis brought about by adherence to outdated conceptual models.[57] One example is reductionism, the conception of reality in which matter is believed to be the basis of all existence and the material world is seen as a multitude of separate parts assembled into a huge "machine." Based on the mathematical theory of Isaac Newton (1642-1727), the philosophy of René Descartes (1596-1650), and the scientific methodology of Francis Bacon (1561-1626), reductionism assumes that complex phenomena can always be understood by reducing them to their basic building blocks and interacting mechanisms.[58] Under the reductionist paradigm, humans' concept of nature devolved from that of living organism to machine, and the predominant value system came to be based on the domination and control of nature rather than respect for and harmony with the natural world.[59]

Capra notes,

> [Reductionism] has become so deeply ingrained in our culture that it has often been identified with the scientific method. The other sciences accepted the mechanistic and reductionistic views of classical physics as the correct description of reality and modeled their own theories accordingly. Whenever psychologists, sociologists, or economists wanted to be scientific, they naturally turned toward the basic concepts of Newtonian physics.
>
> In the twentieth century, however, physics has gone through several conceptual revolutions that clearly reveal the limitations of the mechanistic world view and lead to an organic, ecological view of the world which shows great similarities to the views of mystics of all ages and traditions. The universe is no longer seen as a machine, made up of a multitude of separate objects, but appears as a harmonious indivisible whole; a network of dynamic relationships that include the human observer and his or her consciousness in an essential way.[60]

The paradigm shift described by Capra and others, which views the interrelated systems of the universe as functioning inseparably, is a profound change from the static, seventeenth-century view of life.[61]

Given that Western social sciences have also evolved largely through the reductionist paradigm, the work of those in the field of new physics affirms the application of the holistic approach to the social sciences as well.[62] Indeed, from the holistic perspective, the boundaries between "separate disciplines" are often quite blurred.[63]

Reductionism (which is actually a subset of the holistic paradigm because it is one way to approach things among the gamut of possibilities) has manifested itself in a host of beneficial ways, including cures for many diseases, life-saving surgical techniques, and technological marvels such as lasers, computers, and space stations. But now it is necessary that we acknowledge holism. Capra writes,

> Physicists . . . can provide the scientific background to the changes in attitudes and values that our society so urgently needs. In a culture dominated by science, it will be much easier to convince our social institutions that fundamental changes are necessary if we can give our arguments a scientific basis. This is what physicists can now provide. Modern physics can show the other sciences that scientific thinking does not necessarily have to be reductionist and mechanistic, that holistic and ecological views are also scientifically sound.[64]

The holistic framework "is not only scientific but is in agreement with the most advanced scientific theories of physical reality," Capra adds.[65] Perhaps for the first time, a scientifically valid rationale exists for the holistic paradigm "based on awareness of the essential interrelatedness and interdependence of all phenomena—physical, biological, psychological, social, and cultural."[66] The evidence generated by modern physics both heralds and reflects the validity of the paradigm shift. Knowledge of such objective rationales for holism[67] will also help educators refute charges that they are introducing a new type of "religion" into schools.

In addition to its application in the sciences and in the field of alternative energy, the paradigm shift is evident in healthcare through nutrition, acupuncture, biofeedback, alternative birth centers, visualization techniques, motivational and wellness programs, and so on. As demonstrated by increasing appearances of the terms "whole" and "holistic" in mainstream media, general awareness of the paradigm shift is expanding.

Holistic approaches have been developed in virtually every field of human endeavor. Concerning the holistic paradigm as it applies to medicine, Robert O. Becker, M.D., and Gary Selden write in *The Body Electric,*

> None of our textbooks could tell us the how and why of healing. They explained the basics of scientific medicine—anatomy, biochemistry, bacteriology, pathology, and physiology—each dealing with one aspect of the human body and its discontents. Within each subject the body was further subdivided into systems. The chemistry of muscle and bone, for example, was taught separately from that of the digestive and nervous systems. The same approach is used today, for fragmentation is the only way to deal with a complexity that would otherwise be overwhelming. The strategy works perfectly for understanding spaceships, computers, or other complicated machines, and it's very useful in biology. However, it leads to the reductionist assumption that once you understand the parts, you understand the whole. That approach ultimately fails in the study of living things— hence the widespread demand for an alternative holistic medicine—for life is like no machine humans have ever built: It's always more than the sum of its parts.[68]

Transposed to the social sphere, holism becomes apparent as a rebalancing of values and attitudes that have become distorted— moving from aggressive to responsive, from predominantly masculine to a balance with the feminine, from competitive toward cooperative, from primarily rational toward intuitive, from analyzing toward synthesizing.[69] These are not either/or dichotomies, as nature, an ever-present model for wholeness, reveals.

An important caveat about paradigms: defining the universe according to one system of reality will always fall short. Totality cannot be compressed by mere words into a tidy matrix such as

"holistic or reductionist." These terms are only conceptual represen-
tations. Any categorization overlooks the inherent variability and
subtleties of life.

Addressing the question of whether the world is better understood through holism or reductionism, the Pulitzer Prize–winning
author Douglas R. Hofstadter provides the ancient Zen answer,
mu (nothing, not any). This rejects the premise of the question,
which is that one or the other must be chosen, and indicates that
there is a larger context into which both holistic and reductionist
explanations fit.[70] Capra notes that "ontological levels, like all other
concepts, ultimately are *maya* [deception, illusion, appearance]. The
way in which we divide reality is illusory and relative, and, as we
would say in science, approximate."[71]

The fact remains that the reductionist world view and approach
to learning is still the predominant model in schools and teacher
education programs. Fixed in place before one's enrollment into the
school system and continually reinforced, the reductionist paradigm
is rarely, if ever, identified. When paradigms are discussed it is
generally from a theoretical standpoint only. So amidst all of the
reductionist "trees" being thrown at children, when do they have the
opportunity to perceive the forest? Most adults, as well, do not yet
understand the significance of the whole. Teaching about holism is
one remedy. As Capra observes, "Our society, our universities, our
corporations, our economy, our technology, our politics are all struc-
tured according to the old Cartesian paradigm. We need the shift."[72]

PRACTICAL APPLICATIONS

Two primary aspects of awakening to wholeness are: (a) personally
learning about and connecting with the whole, and (b) investigating
holistic strategies and tangible "artifacts" (a term Fuller used) that
have practical and timely application in the world.

Personally Learning about and Connecting with the Whole

Uncovering the inherent relation of one's inner world with the whole of life is immensely rewarding. As creatures of wholeness, we always resonate to some degree when recognizing something truly of the whole.

When education is holistic—interpersonal and relevant to *what is*—students' interest is maintained and discipline problems evaporate, as many classroom teachers can confirm. The curriculum comes alive when students explore holistic interconnections, not just individual fragments. The emotional connection with the subject matter and the teacher is of paramount importance in learning. When teachers and students spark an egalitarian, interpersonal association, education becomes more lighthearted and meaningful for everyone concerned, creating a yearning for further exploration.

Initially, some teachers may resist examining philosophical concepts such as holistic orientation, preferring traditional approaches to the curriculum. This is to be expected because the quest for objectivity is one of the foundations of education and today's teachers are creations of the existing system.

Some educators maintain that programs to enhance basic literacy should be the primary focus in education, that teaching the three Rs must continue to be given top priority. Learning the three Rs and various specialized studies is necessary, of course, but the mastering of them does not mean an individual will become aware of wholeness. In most classrooms there is little opportunity even to learn that the concept exists. Although not everyone will experience an immediate, consciousness-altering, mystical sense of union with all that is, there are many things about this unity that can be discovered and intuited.

How do holistic principles address practical, nuts-and-bolts education issues such as illiteracy, relevancy, dropout rates, teacher and student burnout, control of public education, vouchers, charter schools, the presence of corporations in schools, overcrowding, violence, testing fairness, or curriculum? Debates over issues such as these have occurred throughout the history of education.

A holistic approach impels us to look beyond specific issues and focus on the larger picture. For example, experience teaches that taking a position on any particular issue usually brings forth, or highlights, an antithesis. Over time, humans have become conditioned to a compartmentalized, oppositional mindset. This leads to compromising rather than optimizing, whereas nature always optimizes, as Buckminster Fuller pointed out.

Polarization is so strong that debates over individual issues in education could continue forever. The same holds true regarding environmental and governmental issues—in fact, issues of every kind. Taking a holistic approach breaks the logjam, providing an order of solutions different from those produced by piecemeal debates. Individual issues become clarified and reframed. What may appear from a reductionist viewpoint to be the most important issues are not usually considered so from the holistic perspective. Similarly, solutions arising from a reductionist viewpoint will generally be recognized as severely limited when evaluated holistically.

For example, forestry policies are most often presented to the public through simplistic, polarized sound-bites ("loggers versus spotted owls" or "business versus the environmentalists"). Considering the increasing severity of our environmental problems, however, the fundamental issues demand a more comprehensive approach. The real issues concern the survival of Earth's forests and humanity itself. Like the proverbial canary in the coal mine, spotted owls are an indicator species pertaining to forest viability. Those who distort the issue into "jobs versus owls" and "erosion of private property rights" obscure what is really happening.

Again we call on Fuller's statement, "To be optimally effective, undertake at outset the most comprehensive task in the most comprehensive and incisively detailed manner." If our goal is to be optimally effective in resolving humanity's most urgent environmental challenges—as well as social and education issues—what is the most comprehensive task?

Fritjof Capra's chart in appendix E highlights the holistic context of global problems pertaining to the environment, economics, government, industrial policy, and ethics. On this chart he states, "Ultimately, these problems appear as different facets of one single crisis, which is a crisis of perception and values." It is indeed a single crisis; yet because people do not generally perceive the interconnectedness of our major global and regional problems, holistic solutions are rarely considered, much less implemented. The need to address this crisis is "the most comprehensive task" facing educators and society at large.

Returning to the question posed above—how do holistic principles address practical issues? They do so by repackaging all issues comprehensively, from the whole to the particulars. Since this approach does not operate from an oppositional mindset, it transcends ideology and encompasses the big picture. It is both noncombative and uncombatable. It is nonpartisan because it implies a viewpoint that includes every viewpoint. With this world view, previously unforeseeable solutions to a wide variety of problems, personal as well as global, can emerge. As synergy manifests itself, unanticipated factors "unpredicted by the behavior of the parts taken separately" (Buckminster Fuller's terminology) come into play.

Holistic education is essential for transforming the human activities that are currently destroying the environment that sustains us. Because so many personal and social problems are rooted in fragmentation and disconnection, cultivating and sharing a holistic orientation is itself ultimately practical—all other applications of holistic principles will flow from the orientation.

Practical Holistic Strategies and Artifacts

In addition to personally learning about and connecting with the whole, another aspect of awakening to wholeness is investigating holistic strategies and tangible artifacts that have timely application in the world. Some areas in which holistic strategies, processes, and/or technologies have already been developed are:

- agriculture, gardening, soils
- atmosphere, air quality
- biodiversity, habitat
- business[73]
- chemicals
- counseling, addiction treatment
- crime, prison and detention systems
- design, construction, shelter
- economics, governance, community,[74] livelihood
- education
- energy, fuels
- ethics, law, conflict resolution
- family issues, cultural survival
- fishing
- forests
- metals, manufacturing
- militarism, military conversion[75]
- nutrition, healthcare, medicine
- oceans, rivers, lakes, streams
- paper, paperboard, and wood products
- population issues, food policy, poverty
- recreation, travel
- sewage, waste management, toxic waste
- transportation, urban planning, land and water policy

This list, which meshes in many ways with Capra's chart, covers most areas of life. As an illustration of the potential impacts of applying holistic strategies, processes, and technologies that already exist for each of these areas, consider the possibilities of just one— paper, paperboard, and wood products.

It is not necessary to chop down forests in order to manufacture paper, because it can be made from alternative sources of raw material such as agricultural fibers including kenaf, industrial hemp, and flax. These sources of pulp are in addition to the vast amount of waste cellulose (described below) including post-consumer waste paper that, instead of being recycled, is still being buried in landfills.[76]

Let us briefly examine one of the agricultural fibers, kenaf (rhymes with *giraffe*). Similar in appearance to sugarcane and bamboo, this fast-growing, woody plant was cultivated in Egypt as early as 4000 B.C.E. It is a member of the hibiscus family and is related to cotton and okra. Able to grow in most regions where farmers produce row crops, it can reach a height of 15 feet in five months (starting from seed) and can annually produce six to ten tons of fiber per acre—two to five times more pulp than an acre of trees.[77]

The timber industry has argued that kenaf is expensive to grow and harvest, and therefore that paper made from it costs too much. But kenaf is actually a low-input crop, and kenaf paper costs more only because of a lack of dedicated processing facilities. Once an infrastructure is in place, the costs will be competitive[78] (even before factoring in environmental benefits). Government giveaways to the timber industry also affect price.

Kenaf is not a panacea; it is only one holistic option for making paper and paperboard products. Along with other fast-growing, low-maintenance tree-free fibers (and fast-growing tree species such as poplar planted on agricultural land using agricultural methods) kenaf does represent an alternative to clearcutting the world's remaining virgin forests. Even if these forests are replanted, the resulting monoculture plantation is no longer a complex forest ecosystem.

Building with "woodless lumber" made from waste cellulose—which is estimated to be generated at a rate of at least 160 million tons per year in the United States alone[79]—is another vital strategy for preserving forests. Waste cellulose includes agricultural residues (the portion of the crop generally considered waste material: straw from wheat, rice, oats, and the like) and materials such as sawdust, urban waste wood, and paper. The Institute for Local Self-Reliance (see appendix C) notes that "sufficient straw alone is available to, in theory, displace as much as 80 percent of our wood-based construction materials."[80] This single holistic option has monumental ramifications.

By definition, any strategy that is holistic supports all other holistic strategies, opening the way for synergy. Holistic strategies are continually being developed; one can learn about many of them through the resources appearing in this book, the Internet, and other avenues.[81] Those interested in practical classroom applications of holism can examine the philosophies and practices of Montessori schools and Waldorf schools (which is not meant as an endorsement of all Montessori and Waldorf schools) and other holistic learning centers. Various educators have described holistic ways to approach teaching, curriculum, child development, and the classroom environment. Works by some of them are listed in appendix B.

No single reference source could include all practical applications of the holistic approach. Since few courses about holism can currently be found in traditional education venues, exploring it necessitates self-directed study. Many videos, audiotapes, and other educational materials are available. Consulting the resources appearing in appendixes B and C will lead to many others.[82]

It is fitting that personal initiative and research are required to discover practical applications in each area of interest. This process can help one learn about wholeness. The reverse is also true: learning about the "subject" of wholeness in general reveals specific practical applications. As one creates holistic strategies, vital information and significant personal realizations invariably emerge, serving as an impetus to learn more.

VALUING THE WHOLE

To be optimally effective in any endeavor requires that one take full advantage of synergy. This happens automatically when one adopts a holistic attitude and undertakes holistic strategies. What could inspire us, individually and collectively, to adopt such an attitude? *Valuing the whole.*

Paradoxically, one needs to see value in the whole in order to have a holistic attitude, yet it's the attitude in the first place that leads one to value the whole. This is a situation in which intuition and conscious decision are called for. A much-needed secular (as well as interdenominational) touchstone for helping educators distinguish the relative virtues of a particular teaching method or curriculum is whether it values the whole.

One question posed earlier asked what unifying ethic could benefit people worldwide. Again the response is *valuing the whole.* Examining whether a given action or policy considers the whole provides an inclusive measure for evaluating the relative merits of actions or policies in any domain—including government, industry, the environment, education, and personal issues. Is a specific policy supportive of life processes? Does a particular activity, philosophy, or counseling method point to wholeness? Does the solution support humanity as a whole without discounting any segment of society or the environment?

From a perspective of valuing the whole, the multitude of personal and collective issues are seen in a different light. Despite the varying agendas of individuals, families, tribes, nationalities, religions, political organizations, and special interest groups, this philosophy emphasizes our common ground. Creating the opposite of fragmentation and polarization, it provides a powerful and compassionate context for personal and planetary evolution.

Taking the parts-to-whole approach, in contrast, we never reach the whole because we become mired in the infinitude of parts. Society's blindness to the whole has exhausted many of the planet's ecosystems and caused great suffering. Continually finding, subdividing, and reselling more *parts* has enabled the extraction of "maximum value" from Earth—a flawed economic system that ignores repercussions to the whole.

THE ROLE OF INTUITION

While most educational materials are presented in linear form (e.g., through writings, lectures, audio/video recordings, and television), connecting with wholeness and valuing the whole arise intuitively through such activities as communing with nature, meditation, contemplation, service, and play. Relevant definitions of intuition are: (a) direct perception of truth independent of any reasoning process, immediate apprehension; (b) a keen and quick insight; and (c) pure, untaught, noninferential knowledge.[83] The philosopher and spiritual teacher J. Krishnamurti (1895-1986) described intuition as "intelligence highly awakened, . . . which is the only true guide in life."[84]

Intuition can help us find our way through the brambles of fragmentation and cognitive discord. Unfortunately, some people mistake deranged thought for intuition, providing an excuse for just about anything (including acts of terrorism). Therefore, to be useful, intuition must be unclouded, informed, and sensibly interpreted. Who is to be the judge of these factors? Learning about and experiencing wholeness can provide personal clarity.

Although objective rationales for holism exist, words and reason are ultimately inadequate for illuminating wholeness. The ability to connect instantly with the whole remains constant, however, because humans are entities *of* the whole.

Wholeness is the sea in which we exist. But even to comment on this sea creates a duality. Our entire perceptual approach has generally been based on duality, separating the observer and the observed, a theme that is addressed in chapter 3.

To summarize, these features of holism can serve as reference points to discern, evaluate, and enhance every subject, activity, issue, curriculum, platform, goal, or domain of life:

Synergy: Commencing with the whole system, look for synergistic connections within the given area and with related areas. Investigate ways to optimize potentials for synergy.

Whole-to-parts orientation: Identify the big picture before proceeding to the parts. Discover the holistic orientation.

The invisible realm: Investigate invisible connections. Where do they come into play? How do they relate to the more tangible aspects?

The paradigm shift: Explore how thinking in terms of evolving paradigms sheds light on the area of concern. This provides a helpful context for communicating the holistic approach to others.

Practical applications: Discover practical applications of holistic philosophy including methods for holistic teaching. A holistic orientation is intrinsically practical since applications and solutions will arise from it.

Valuing the whole: Cherish the whole for its own sake and with respect to all subjects, activities, and relationships.

The role of intuition: Recognize the central importance of intuition in awakening to wholeness, in discerning the need for holistic solutions, and in implementing those solutions.

What Kind of World?

Do we want wild salmon in the world or not? Should we save the rain forests, the magnificent Siberian tiger? Is the world meant only for the wealthy and those who serve them? Is it intended only for particular religious sects, or do all people, life forms, and habitats have worth? The kind of world we want will determine how we should be educating ourselves and our children.

Awakening to wholeness enhances the ability to differentiate valid and desirable options from hype and disinformation regarding the environmental crisis, world economy, and every other collective and personal matter. As we learn about the whole, we become more conscious of our available choices and less prone to being manipulated. Holism is not just another philosophy among many. As stated earlier, it is a metaphilosophy that can be used as a *tool for discerning* all philosophies, and everything else.

In the context of Buckminster Fuller's advice, how can a person determine what actions are "optimally effective" for a given situation? Learning about and experiencing wholeness are essential. What are some "comprehensive tasks" that one might undertake? These appear, unique to each individual, as people come into holistic awareness and implement holistic principles in their lives.

What would constitute a "comprehensive and incisively detailed manner" for accomplishing such tasks? When one operates from a holistic orientation, insights arise. Since education, economic, political, and religious systems dominated by reductionist beliefs lie at the root of many environmental and social ills, it is necessary that we examine our paradigms and educate ourselves holistically.

Which plan is best? Which world view? The answer must be personal. Awakening to wholeness is a starting point for discerning the answers to these questions and creating strategies relevant to one's own life.

Attacks on the planet's life-support systems are among the most critical manifestations of humanity's widespread ignorance about wholeness. In this age of space travel, instant global communication, and internationally overlapping environmental situations, the Earth and all its interconnected life forms—indeed, all creation—present an obvious and accessible unifying vision. It is past time for wholeness to be considered a basic "subject" in education and everyday discourse.

There is no returning to isolationism. As supranational corporations and the globalized economic system predominate, national political perspectives have become moot in many respects. It would be simplistic to infer that education in the "subject" of wholeness can resolve every personal, social, and environmental issue; however, this is certainly a pivotal strategy toward personal and planetary well-being.

It has been said that peace in the world is not possible until peace has been attained within one's own heart. In its most basic sense, holistic education is the process of becoming whole. This awakening also provides a pattern for developing the consensus required to stop the assault on the environment, improve living conditions world-wide, and create an enlightened global civilization. Because holistic education is *education about education,* it is a golden key for achieving personal and collective potential in life.

CHAPTER 2

Buckminster Fuller

The greater complex is never predicted by the parts of the lesser complex. Therefore, . . . to learn anything you must start with the whole—with Universe. Comprehension of the whole alone leads to discovery of the significant intercomplementary functions to be played by the parts.

R. BUCKMINSTER FULLER

Fuller in Context

Buckminster Fuller's Presidential Medal of Freedom citation describes him as "a true Renaissance Man, and one of the greatest minds of our times."[1] He has also been referred to as "the Leonardo da Vinci of our times" and "the planet's friendly genius."[2] Who was this man and why is his work so important to the "subject" of wholeness? *The Encyclopedia of the Environment* provides an overview:

> American architect and inventor. Richard Buckminster Fuller [1895-1983] was an early champion of the principle of synergy and a pioneer in the exploration of whole systems and their relevance to understanding and addressing the problems of Earth. Decades before others, he drew pictures of a "One Town World," and developed a distortion-free world map to illustrate our "one-world island in a one-world ocean." He coined the phrase "Spaceship Earth" early in the 1950s before NASA photographed the planet. Between 1927 and the 1960s, as part of his ongoing research, he made inventories of the world's resources, trends, and needs, concluding that humanity has the resources and technological capacity to support 100 percent of the human population, long before others even asked the question. He extolled the importance of concepts like recycling, years before they achieved fashion. He designed and prototyped "artifacts," i.e., inventions, such as mass-produced shelter, developed to address specific global problems. He was the author of 28 books, and recipient of dozens of awards, including . . . 47 honorary doctorate degrees in arts, sciences, engineering, and humanities.[3]

A primary assumption underlying Buckminster Fuller's philosophy is that Earth is here for all. He sought to raise the standard of living for everyone. Fuller demonstrated that along with the specific knowledge, the technology is already available that can help ensure humanity's continued survival on planet Earth. He was aware that harmful by-products from unholistic uses of technology could eventually ruin Earth for human habitation. Fuller dedicated his life to providing alternatives to this scenario.

Buckminster Fuller's work is of central importance because it is relevant to so many aspects of life. For more than 55 years, he explored the world holistically and taught about his discoveries. A brilliant inventor, engineer, geometrician, poet, architect/designer, educator, cartographer, and philosopher, he produced numerous artifacts and strategies that apply the holistic paradigm to everyday concerns.

Early in his career, Fuller realized that mere persuasion would not convince people to think and act holistically. Instead, he resolved to "reform the environment, not the humans" by translating principles found in nature's designs into practical applications for the benefit of all.[4]

Nature employs the most efficient, optimized designs. Fuller demonstrated that by emulating the design processes of nature, people could free themselves from many drudgeries (among other benefits), leaving more time for creativity and enjoyment. By developing artifacts and strategies that are inherently educational and that do not require philosophical interpretation, he hoped to circumvent the politicization of his work.

Learning the basics of Fuller's philosophy of "comprehensivity" will enhance one's ability to connect with the whole and to act in accord with it. Wherever feasible in this chapter, Buckminster Fuller's own words are used to present his philosophy. It bears mentioning that his language is often extremely rich and dense, and portions may initially seem difficult to follow.

"Education for Comprehensivity"[5]

Buckminster Fuller observed that many undesirable environmental, economic, and social conditions stem from outmoded thinking and behavior patterns (antiquated paradigms). He believed that we can overcome the critical challenges facing Earth's inhabitants only by becoming educated "comprehensively."

> The Dark Ages still reign over all humanity, and the depth and persistence of this domination are only now becoming clear.
>
> This Dark Ages prison has no steel bars, chain, or locks. Instead, it is locked by misorientation and built of misinformation. Caught up in a plethora of conditioned reflexes and driven by the human ego, both warden and prisoner attempt meagerly to compete with God. All are intractably skeptical of what they do not understand.
>
> We are powerfully imprisoned in these Dark Ages simply by the terms in which we have been conditioned to think.[6]

One outmoded thinking pattern Fuller referred to is the belief that specialized education is always preferable. He wrote,

> The general theory of education at present starts students off with elementary components and gradually increases the size of the complex of components with which the student will be concerned. The scheme is to go from the particular toward the whole but never to reach the whole.[7]

"Education for comprehensivity," in contrast, starts with the whole and then progresses to the particulars and their interconnections. Fuller pointed out that in nature overspecialization leads to extinction. "Generalized adaptability is needed to cope with large changes in the environment," he said, emphasizing that our lack of attention to this fact is humanity's "chief peril."[8]

Because it has proved so successful in industry, many remain convinced that the subassemblies (parts-to-whole) approach is desirable for all fields.[9] But this method presents limitations:

> Going from micro to macro, each more inclusive aspect of Universe is unpredicted by any of its respective subparts taken separately. Universe is a synergy of synergies. It is a corollary of synergy that the known behavior of wholes plus the known behavior of a few of their

parts enables discovery of other parts and their behavioral character-istics. In order to really understand what is going on, we have to abandon starting with parts, and we must work instead from the whole to the particulars.[10]

Viewed from this perspective, the fields of mathematics, geometry, physics, and chemistry, which are not separate in nature, would be seen simply as *"one* field: 'how Nature builds.'"[11] E. J. Applewhite, Fuller's friend and collaborator on *Synergetics* and *Synergetics 2,* notes that, to Fuller, "there is always only one topic: the universe—whole systems."[12] Fuller said,

> Becoming deliberately expansive instead of contractive, we ask, *"How* do we think in terms of *wholes?"* If it is true that the bigger the think-ing becomes the more lastingly effective it is, we must ask, "How big can we think?"[13]

This perspective suggests a philosophical frame of reference far dif-ferent from that generally employed in education.

To Fuller, the opposite of a specialist is not a generalist (one who has knowledge in a variety of areas) but a "comprehensivist" who values the whole and has an all-encompassing, holistic perception of reality. With this approach, interconnections and practical applica-tions of holistic principles can be seen. It is necessary to gain a sense of the whole in order even to know what a part is.

Fuller stated that shifting "from a Newtonian static norm to an Einsteinian all-motion norm" is the most important event of our times.[14] Applying his guide for optimum effectiveness ("undertake at outset the most comprehensive task in the most comprehensive and incisively detailed manner"), Fuller's self-selected task was to help make the world work for 100 percent of humanity in the shortest possible time through spontaneous cooperation, without environmental offense, and without causing disadvantage to any-one.[15] He taught that humanity's continued survival on the planet requires comprehensive solutions and that nature's methodology provides the best model.[16]

Generalized Principles

According to Buckminster Fuller, the essence of becoming a comprehensivist lies in learning and applying what he termed "generalized principles."

> Above all I sought to comprehend the principles of eternally regenerative Universe and to discover human functioning therein, thereby to discover nature's governing complexes of generalized principles and to employ these principles in the development of the specific artifacts that would benefit humanity's fulfillment of its essential functioning in the cosmic scheme.[17]

Generalized principles are "the synergetic rules that evolution is employing and trying to make clear to us."[18] These principles are "the infinitely accommodative laws of the intellectual integrity governing universe," rules that hold true without exception—eternal laws of nature.[19] In using the phrase "intellectual integrity governing universe," Fuller explained that generalized principles are not human inventions.[20] They are valid in every sphere. For example, "doing more with less" can apply to such heterogeneous fields as design, construction, agriculture, energy production, music, art, and athletics. These vital holistic principles include the following:

SYNERGY

Buckminster Fuller believed that the investigation of synergy (introduced in the first chapter) should occupy a central position in education. He was among those responsible for bringing the term into popular usage. Dictionaries define synergy as "combined action or operation," "cooperative action," "combined or correlated force." Fuller stated, "Synergy means behavior of whole systems unpredicted by the behavior of their parts taken separately."[21] He explained,

> There is nothing in one atom per se that predicts that atoms will combine to form chemical compounds. One atom does not predict anything, let alone the existence of another atom or combinations of one known atom with an as-yet-unknown other atom. . . .
> There is nothing in chemical compounds per se that predicts biological protoplasm. There is nothing in biological protoplasm per se

that predicts camels and palm trees and the intercomplementary interexchange of the waste gases given off by them. There is nothing in the exchange of these gases that predicts galaxies and stars.[22]

As Fuller pointed out, the universe itself is a "synergy of synergies," and "synergy alone explains the eternally regenerative integrity of Universe."[23]

EPHEMERALIZATION

This is the process of "doing more with less."[24] One example Fuller used was the Telstar—a type of communications satellite that weighed only 500 pounds yet outperformed 75,000 tons of transoceanic copper cable.[25]

According to Fuller, "efficiency ephemeralizes."[26] He offered an illustration with respect to the circumnavigation of Earth: "wooden sailing ship, three years; steel beam ship, three weeks; aluminum airplane, three days; metal-structured rocket capsule [i.e., spacecraft], ninety minutes."[27] The advent of fiber optics and advances in microchip capability provide other clear examples of doing more with less.

Fuller's geodesic dome is a manifestation of this principle. Since geodesic domes have a much higher strength-to-weight ratio than traditional cubical buildings covering the same volume of space, they require far less building material, weighing approximately 3 percent of the weight of a conventional building of equal span.[28] Domes in general are able to enclose more volume with less surface area than any other type of construction; however, a *geodesic* dome is unique. *Random House Webster's Unabridged Dictionary,* second edition, defines it as

> a light, domelike structure developed by R. Buckminster Fuller to combine the properties of the tetrahedron and the sphere and consisting essentially of a grid of compression or tension members lying upon or parallel to great circles running in three directions in any given area, the typical form being the projection upon a sphere of an icosahedron, the triangular faces of which are filled with a symmetrical triangular, hexagonal, or quadrangular grid.

One of the most famous geodesic domes (actually a three-quarter sphere) is the U.S. pavilion built for the 1967 World's Fair in Montreal. Another is the dome at Disney's EPCOT Center in Orlando, Florida. Small, unroofed geodesic domes for climbing can be found on children's playgrounds everywhere. Geodesic domes are relatively inexpensive, mass-producible, and can be constructed from a variety of materials. They can be built to withstand winds of 200 mph or more and to be earthquake proof (assuming the foundation remains intact), yet they can be light and strong enough for delivery by air; for disaster relief, thousands of family-sized geodesic domes could be delivered by cargo plane. Very large geodesic domes can be delivered by suspending them from a helicopter or blimp. Geodesic domes of any size can be quickly assembled on site.

In addition to being a feasible solution to the world's housing shortage, geodesic domes could also span neighborhoods or whole cities —for instance, in the event of severe climate disruption. (This would necessitate, of course, that vehicles, homes, and businesses be non-polluting.)[29]

Given that the most efficient designs are found in nature, Fuller based his geodesic designs on the mathematical principles nature employs. Geodesic dome-like structures can be observed in crystals, virus and protein molecules, eyeballs, bony cells, fundamental particles, micro sea structures, and other formations.[30]

One dramatic example of a natural geodesic structure is carbon-60, a third allotrope of carbon (in addition to diamond and graphite) discovered in 1985 by Dr. Richard Smalley, Sir Harold Kroto, and Dr. Robert Curl, for which they were awarded the 1996 Nobel Prize in chemistry. Named Buckminsterfullerene in Fuller's honor, this molecule is often called a Buckyball. Extremely resilient, it displays 60 carbon atoms arranged in a spherical geodesic pattern. The discovery of Buckminsterfullerene, and related molecules that were subsequently found, has generated considerable scientific research into possible applications for them as superconductors and industrial lubricants, and in such fields as nanotechnology and plastics.[31]

"Doing more with less" does not imply a lower standard of living. In fact, the opposite is true. Infinite synergistic possibilities will emerge as our production and consumption patterns begin to embody this principle, since it can be applied to every domain.

Fuller taught that the principle of ephemeralization renders obsolete the Malthusian[32] assumption of the inherent inadequacy of life support on Earth (which is not meant to diminish the overpopulation issue). Refutation of such gloomy economic models was a recurring theme in Fuller's work.

> Economists traditionally try to maximize what you have, but the idea that you could go from wire to wireless or from visible structuring to invisible alloy structuring did not occur to them at all. It was outside their point of view—beyond their range of vision. Economists are specialists trained to look only at one particular thing.[33]

Fuller's book *Critical Path* contains a wealth of practical applications pertaining to ephemeralization. For example, *acceleration* of ephemeralization is a phenomenon that constitutes a subject in itself. To illustrate: Fuller realized that, over time, as scrap metals and other recyclables are returned (and returned again) for re-alloying and re-manufacturing, there is a progressively greater performance per unit of material, energy, and time. The fact that ephemeralization accelerates has enormous environmental, social, and economic implications.

As J. Baldwin, author of *BuckyWorks: Buckminster Fuller's Ideas for Today,* points out, "Ephemeralization is not something you add to a design, it occurs naturally as the result of applied natural principles. It's more of an attitude than a strategy."[34] As with synergy, ephemeralization is a potential that can be focused for the common betterment, including the restoration and preservation of environmental life-support systems.

PRECESSION

Precession is a phenomenon of physics that pertains to momentum, angle, and velocity. In *A Fuller Explanation: The Synergetic Geometry of R. Buckminster Fuller,* Amy C. Edmondson defines the term and provides a concise explanation of Fuller's expanded use of it:

> Two or more systems in motion with respect to each other involving 90-degree turn. In addition to its meaning in physics—describing a complex motion of a rotating body in response to an applied torque—Fuller employs this word (as well as his own "interprecessing") to refer to two geometrical systems which, oriented perpendicularly to each other, reveal a new system or geometric relationship.[35]

In a prose poem Fuller wrote, *"Precession* is the behavioral inter-relationship / of remote and differently velocitied, / differently directioned, / and independently moving bodies / upon one another's separate motions / and motion interpatternings."[36] Stated another way, it is "the integrated effect of bodies in motion on other bodies in motion."[37] For example, when a stone is dropped into water, a circular wave is generated in a plane perpendicular to the line of the stone, and "the outwardly expanding circular wave generates (at ninety degrees) a vertical wave that in turn generates an additional horizontally and outwardly expanding wave, and so on."[38] Similarly, Fuller

Drawings from Critical Path, *1981*

explained, "Despite the 180-degree gravitational pull of the in-motion Sun upon the in-motion Earth, precession makes Earth orbit around the Sun in a direction that is at ninety degrees—i.e., at a right angle—to the direction of the Sun's gravitational pull upon Earth."[39]

> The greatest lesson that nature is now trying to teach humanity is that when the bumblebee goes after its honey, it inadvertently pollinizes the vegetation, which pollinization, accomplished at 90 degrees to the bumblebee's aimed activity, constitutes part of the link-up of the great ecological regeneration . . . of life on our planet. . . .[40]

> So, too, do all the mobile creatures of Earth cross-fertilize all the different rooted botanicals in one or another precessional (right-angled), inadvertent way.[41]

> What humans called the side effects of their conscious drives in fact produced the main ecological effects of generalized technological regeneration. I therefore assumed that what humanity rated as "side effects" are nature's *main effects.* I adopted the precessional "side effects" as my prime objective.[42]

> In [an] indirect way, humanity is at present being taught by
> nature that its armament making as a way to make a living for itself
> is inadvertently producing side effects of gained knowledge of how to
> do ever more with ever less and how, therewith, to render all the
> resources on earth capable of successful support of all humanity. The
> big lesson . . . is called *precession*.[43]

Like other generalized principles, precession provides a point of
entry for examining the whole of any subject or activity. Fuller
taught that "precession is regenerative,"[44] which holds true in both
the physical and the psychological realms:

> What nature told humanity chromosomally was, "I'm hungry, my
> kids are hungry; I'm cold, my kids are cold. Go after that food and
> that coat. They cost money—go after money. They say you have to
> earn it. OK, I'll earn it." Buzz, buzz, honey-money bee. No human
> chromosomes say make the world work for everybody—only mind
> can tell you that.[45]

> So preoccupied with its honey-money bumbling has society been
> that the ninety-degree side effects of the century-old science of
> ecology remained long unnoticed by the populace. Ecology is the
> world-around complex intercomplementation of all the biological
> species' regenerative intercyclings with nature's geological and
> meteorological transformation recyclings. Society discovered ecology
> only when its economically sidewise discards of unprofitable sub-
> stances became so prodigious as to pollutingly frustrate nature's
> regenerative mainstream intersupport. Society's surprise "discovery"
> of ecology in the 1960s constituted its as-yet-realistically-unre-
> sponded-to discovery of nature's main effects—ergo, of precession.[46]

Learning to recognize and value events and activities with
respect to precession is an important element of holistic education.[47] While some connections are obvious, others are more subtle.
Fuller wrote,

> *Mass attraction* is to *precession* / as a *single note* is to *music*. / Precession
> is *angularly accelerating*, / *regeneratively progressive* / *mass attraction*.

> Because the sun's planets / did not fall into one another / Kepler's
> discovery of their elliptic orbiting / as well as the solar system's
> motion / relative to other star groups / of the Galactic Nebula / are
> all and only accounted for / by *precession*.

Precession is uniquely dependent / upon the entirely unexplained, / ergo mystically occurring, / omnimotions of Universe / successfully hypothesized by Einstein / in contradistinction / to Newton's assumed / a priori cosmic norm of "at rest."

Precession is a *second-degree synergy* / because it is not predicted by mass attraction / considered only by itself. . . .[48]

ETERNALLY REGENERATIVE UNIVERSE

Fuller referred to entropy as "the inexorable course of the gradual running down of the energy of the Universe."[49] This phenomenon is taken into account by the second law of thermodynamics, which, stated another way, says that "all physical processes lead to a decrease in the availability of the energy involved."[50] Fuller emphasized that entropy has a complimentary phase, *syntropy*, which serves as a balance. He coined this word because the term "anti-entropy" has limitations; he taught that there is no "anti" in nature, only balance. Fuller explained,

> The entropic Sun radiation is constantly being impounded by the syntropic photosynthesis of the vegetation and converted from random radiation receipts into beautiful, orderly molecular structures (matter), with other living creatures and organisms in turn consuming the vegetation-produced molecules and thereby syntropically "growing" physically by themselves, producing large numbers of chemically orderly molecules. We observe this great syntropic operation pattern to be manifest in the natural ecology of our planet.[51]

He stated how human activity contributes to this process:

> By and large the function of life on the planet is designed to be syntropic—to impound the radiation, conserve it, and use it to produce further syntropic functioning in overall support of the syntropic integrity of eternally regenerative Universe. The tendencies of many human beings—wanting to cultivate the soil, to care for the animals, the drive of artists to create, of artisans to build, of inventors to invent and develop time- and trouble-savers for others—are all manifests of the designed-in syntropic propensities of humans. The generous, compassionate propensity of humans is primarily syntropic.[52]

As with every aspect of Fuller's teaching, both physical and metaphysical components are involved. Fuller observed,

> Mind possibly may serve as the essential, anti-entropic (syntropic) function for eternally conserving the omni-interaccommodative, non-simultaneous, and only partially overlapping, omni-intertransforming, self-regenerating scenario, which we speak of as "Universe."
>
> . . . If so, it will have to be accomplished by apprehending, comprehending, and teleologically employing the metaphysical, weightless, omni-intercooperative generalized principles of Universe in strategically effective degree and within a critical time limit.
>
> This can be accomplished in progressively more effective ways. . . . The task of metaphysical intellect is to cooperate with evolution as a major syntropic factor by collecting, sorting, and symmetrically combining information into ever more advantageous and orderly patterns, i.e., designs, to offset the physical Universe's macrocosmic proclivities of becoming locally ever more dissynchronous, asymmetric, diffuse, and multiplyingly expansive.[53]

Learning about "eternally regenerative Universe"[54] and other generalized principles helps us to appreciate the exquisite, intelligent, and coherent functioning of the whole. Fuller affirmed that generalized principles are *a priori*.

> Since all the cosmic-scale inventing and designing is accomplishable only by intellect, and since it is not by the intellect of humans, it is obviously that of the eternal intellectual integrity we call God.[55]

All aspects of Buckminster Fuller's work are interrelated and for full impact must be regarded in their holistic context. Every entrance point to his work—generalized principles, artifacts such as the geodesic dome, synergetics (discussed below), his philosophy of education, for example—relates directly to every other facet. Thus, it does not make sense to investigate holistic subject matter reductionistically. If Fuller's work is approached by focusing only on isolated elements, the crucial perspective—his vision of wholeness and synergy—is lost.

Universe apparently is omnisynergetic. No single part of experience will ever be able to explain the behavior of the whole. The more experience one has, the more opportunity there is to discover the synergetic effects, such as to be able to discern a generalized principle, for instance. Then discovery of a plurality of generalized principles permits the discovery of the synergetic effects of their complex interactions. The synergetic metaphysical effect produced by the interaction of the known family of generalized principles is probably what is spoken of as wisdom.[56]

Spaceship Earth

The image of Spaceship Earth is a multidimensional symbol for wholeness. This term was originated by Fuller in 1951 to convey the sense of Earth as a system in which everything is interconnected. Earth's inhabitants are travelers orbiting the sun, interdependent upon each other, the craft, and its universe-matrix for survival. The spaceship, both literally and metaphorically, presents a comprehensive framework for addressing issues regarding ecology, energy, agriculture, economics, and other areas of global concern.

THE FULLER PROJECTION

Buckminster Fuller invented a new map of the world, which he described as follows:

> It was to provide a satisfactory means for humanity to see correctly the entire surface of the globe all at the same time that the Dymaxion Sky-Ocean Projection [renamed the Fuller Projection in 1992] was designed. With it, for the first time in history, humans can see their whole planet Earth's geography displayed on one flat surface without any visible distortion in shape or relative size of any of its data and without any breaks in its continental contour—that is, the whole world surface is viewable simultaneously as one-world island of unbroken contour in one-world ocean.[57]

Although a globe is the least distorted type of map, it doesn't allow the entire planet to be viewed at once. The pattern of the flat map is an unhinged icosahedron skillfully configured so that no land mass is bisected along the triangular cut lines.

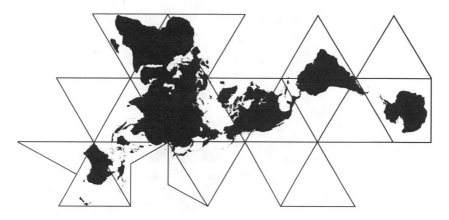

Designed in 1930 and published by *Life* magazine in 1943,[58] the Dymaxion™ Sky-Ocean World Map is also known as the Spaceship Earth Map. "Dymaxion" (a compound of "dynamic," "maximum," and "ion") refers to a structural/mathematical principle pertaining to "maximum gain advantage from the minimal energy input"— doing more with less.[59] This term also applies to many of Fuller's other designs, the Dymaxion House and Dymaxion Car, for example.

The concept that all humans live on one island has important implications for education, as well as for fields such as social psychology and international relations. Sharing the same island with people of other cultures feels quite different from envisioning them across a huge ocean or in another hemisphere. The Fuller Projection illustrates the statement by the physician and educator Lewis Thomas (1913-1993) that "[Earth] is *most* like a single cell."[60] Educators find the Fuller Projection an invaluable addition to the classroom.

THE GEOSCOPE

Another of Fuller's revolutionary ideas was the Geoscope, which he described as "a gossamer, open trusswork spherical structure wherewith humanity can see and read all the spherical data of the Earth's geography as seen from either its inside or its outside and in its proper interorientation within the theater of local Universe events."[61]

Continents are represented with transparent material (e.g., screening) so a person standing inside a Geoscope at night can view the stars. When a Geoscope is installed, its latitudes and longitudes are aligned with Earth's latitude and longitude at the exact point on the planet's surface that is specific to each Geoscope. Therefore, "it will be found that the miniature Earth Geoscope's real omnidirec-

Geoscope, early development, 1952

tional celestial-theater orientation always corresponds exactly with the real omnidirectional celestial-theater orientation of the real planet Earth."[62] Fuller elaborated:

> The situation is similar to that of a small boat mounted rigidly on the davits of the Queen Mary. The small boat takes the same relative angles to the sea as the great ship does. The center of the little earth is only a few thousand miles from that of the big earth, compared to the nearest star's 92 million miles. Parallax [in this case, the apparent displacement of a celestial body due to its being observed from the surface instead of from the center of the earth] sets in the sphere so that when we stand in the center we can see exactly the same things that we would see if we stood at the center of the earth and looked out through more or less transparent continents. If we saw a star over Paris, France in our sphere, that would actually be over real Paris, France. In other words, we had a true planetarium in which we no longer saw sunsets or sunrises, but only the sun, always in zenith to some part of the miniature earth which turned in relation to the sun.[63]

Fuller explained the rationale behind the Geoscope:

> There are many motion patterns such as those of the hands of a clock or of the solar system planets or of the molecules of gas in a pneumatic ball or of atoms or the earth's annual weather that cannot be seen or comprehended by the human eye and brain relay and are therefore inadequately comprehended and dealt with by the human mind.[64]

Elsewhere he described how the Geoscope works:

> Because outwardly of Geoscope's equator what we can see of the starry scene is changing most rapidly and ever less rapidly until, looking out along the polar axis, we observe no change, we get the same feeling as we do looking out the window of a railway car, automobile, or airplane. We see and feel the scene changing as a consequence of our vehicle's motion and not of the scenery's motion. For the first time in human experience Geoscope's mini-Earth spherical structure is clearly seen and felt to be revolving within the theater of Universe, and those holding steady their bodies, head and their eyes and standing at the Geoscope's center, feel-see their Earth revolving within the vast theater of the starry sky.[65]

The Geoscope provides a distinct perception of moving with the Earth—of visually and viscerally experiencing oneness with it.

World Game

Imagine a computerized Fuller Projection half the size of a football field and covered with millions of closely packed, miniature, multi-colored lights (or an extra-large Diamond Vision®–type screen stretched out horizontally). Fuller envisioned using such a map in a great "world logistics game."[66] A computer—programmed with the world's known inventory of resources and needs, detailed demographics, weather patterns, toxic emissions data, and other variables—would be wired to the giant screen so that simulations of various strategies could be observed on a global scale via moving patterns of lights (like the graphics on a Goodyear blimp). At the rate of one second per year, decade, or century, data and events concerning phenomena such as deforestation, topsoil distribution, cloud-cover history, and population migration could be simulated (alone or juxtaposed with other phenomena) in a matter of minutes, revealing significant patterns. For example,

> [one] change to be illustrated is resource transpositioning, such as the shift in geographical location of the world's iron metal from mines of yesterday, much of which is now converted into world-around city buildings, railway tracks, and bridges, all of which latter are scrapped when the buildings or railways become obsolete. Yesterday's buildings and equipment have now become our "highest grade" iron mines. The data covering such epoch shifts may be comprehensively introduced into the computer's memory bank and acceleratingly displayed . . . to be comprehended by any human of sound brain and mind.[67]

In elaborating upon the purpose of playing the World Game, Fuller proposed that

> individuals and teams would undertake to play the World Game with those resources, behaviors, trends, vital needs, developmental desirables, and regenerative inspirations. The players as individuals or teams would each develop their own theory of how to make the total world work successfully for all of humanity. Each individual or team would play a theory through to the end of a predeclared program. It could be played with or without competitors.
>
> The objective of the game would be to explore ways to make it possible for anybody and everybody in the human family to enjoy the total Earth without any human interfering with any other human and without any human gaining advantage at the expense of another.[68]

Fuller also envisioned the World Game being played on a special kind of Geoscope, 200 feet in diameter, covered with miniature, multi-colored lights and computerized like the Fuller Projection described above. To see pictures with details equal to "a fine-screen halftone print," Fuller specified that the viewer should be at least 100 feet from the surface of the Geoscope, "as seen from either the center of the sphere or from the ground outside and 100 feet below."[69] The sphere could also be "a complex of spherically coordinated TV tubes," resulting in "a miniature Earth—the most accurate global representation of our planet ever to be realized."[70]

The optimum Geoscope is designed to make practical an omnidirectional moving picture displayed on the surface of a large sphere for presenting all manner of information relevant to all human affairs as they occur around the whole of our planet, so that the whole world's population can learn for itself how to comprehend the significance of the world-around information as compounded with other powerfully relevant, long-known, and broadcast news and other Geoscope-mounted information.[71]

Fuller provided the following rationale for World Game simulations:

Juxtaposition and overlaying of seemingly unrelated information may produce unexpected and otherwise unimaginable pictures quickly and synergetically.

One of the most fantastic capabilities of the human brain is that of complex pattern recognition. If world-encompassing actions were accelerated, or a facsimile of the action presented within the velocity range of human comprehension, not only would the motion become clearly visible, but also some fundamental principles or heretofore unfamiliar forms of behavior probably would be exposed. The brain quickly correlates such new information with previously acquired data and insight gained from other experiences and adds understanding to the new phenomena being examined. Many of today's seemingly completely new and complex occurrences are in fact relatively simple and are clearly related to other phenomena with which we have learned to deal successfully.

With the Geoscope humanity would be able to recognize formerly invisible patterns and thereby to forecast and plan in vastly greater magnitude than heretofore.[72]

World Game—whether played on the giant Fuller Projection or the Geoscope just described (each computerized and covered with miniature lights, as yet undeveloped) or on a personal computer (see World Game Institute, below)—has considerable practical ramifications not only for education but for fulfilling our obligations to the environment. Such a tool would enable people everywhere to become accurately and apolitically informed about global conditions:

The consequences of various world plans could be computed and projected, using the accumulated history-long inventory of economic, demographic, and sociologic data. All the world data would be dynamically viewable and picturable and relayable by radio [also by television and the Internet] to all the world, so that common consideration in a most educated manner of all world problems by all world people would become a practical everyday, -hour and -minute event.[73]

The new educational technology . . . will of eventual, emergency-emerged, critical necessity come to produce and use the Geoscopes as basic educational tools for acquiring both cosmic and local Universe orientation. . . . Geoscope will spontaneously induce total-Earth, total-humanity viewing significance in regard to all our individual daily experiences. It will spontaneously eliminate nationalistic cerebrating.[74]

Since people cannot be coerced into being conscious of the whole and living in oneness, a key word here is "spontaneously." While environmental policies and school curriculum selections can be politicized, the information received through a Geoscope does not require outside interpretation.

Fuller imagined a Geoscope 200 feet in diameter suspended above the East River in New York City (around 50th Street) from five 300-foot masts so the top of the Geoscope would be level with the top of the United Nations building. Since the geodesic sphere would be relatively light, small diameter cables of high tensile strength could be used for suspension. From a distance the cables would be invisible, and the Geoscope would appear to float in midair above the river. Such a prominent Geoscope could serve as an "everyday facility" of the U.N., computerized to reveal at a glance (via moving patterns of lights) the status of the world.[75] Baldwin illustrates:

The spread of a disease could be displayed dramatically in moving lights. Filling of wetlands, distribution of cotton, mining of gravel, and the shipping of rice could be presented visually in a memorable and understandable way. The locations of surplus food, starving populations, and empty ships could be shown together, perhaps suggesting a remedy.

Bucky was confident World Game would show that international cooperation was so obviously advantageous that war would become unthinkable. Humans could then enter a new phase of their role in Universe.[76]

Another potential use of World Game simulations is to explore various options for energy production and delivery. For example, our current system of centralized electricity production (hydroelectric, nuclear, and fossil fuel–burning plants connected to large-scale electrical distribution grids) could be compared with widespread on-site electricity production from solar energy, wind power, and hydrogen fuel cells, along with the benefits of conservation and high efficiency at the point of use (as with low-energy light bulbs). By simulating the probable consequences of different strategies or combinations thereof, World Game can help us weigh various factors, determine trade-offs, and arrive at optimum solutions for Earth and for all of its inhabitants.

Although the World Game might reveal that a bioregional approach to governance and conservation—as well as a bioregional and point-of-use approach to energy production and agriculture, to mention only a few areas—is the most effective strategy for human survival and well-being, it appears that some sort of world administrative body will still be needed if we are to safeguard the world's biodiversity, atmosphere, oceans, and other environmental life-support systems. Such an administrative body could greatly benefit from data provided by computerized World Game simulations.[77]

Baldwin summarizes, "Of all his inventions and discoveries, Bucky considered World Game to be second only to synergetics as a force for making humans a successful species."[78] Fuller predicted,

> The Geoscope will make possible communication of evolutionary phenomena not hitherto comprehendingly communicable via humans' conceptual faculties regarding their Spaceship Earth's orientation and course of travel amongst the other planets around the Sun, as well as of the comprehensive evolutionary developments occurring around the surface of our Spaceship Earth. . . . Many events about to take place will be dramatically evidenced, as will the avoidability of many events which, if unanticipated by humans, would tend to destroy us all—and on the other hand, if reliably anticipated, will make possible safe and happy continuance.[79]

Although the computerized World Game of Fuller's vision—using a flat screen half the size of a football field or the Geoscope—does not yet exist, the World Game Institute has developed other versions, including one for the Internet, as well as software.

WORLD GAME INSTITUTE

Inspired by Buckminster Fuller, the World Game Institute, located in Philadelphia, is a nonprofit, nonpartisan research and educational organization (see appendix C). This organization conducts World Game Workshops, employing a large (nearly the size of a basketball court), laminated Fuller Projection world map created from U.S. Defense Department jet navigational charts. The titles of the Institute's workshops convey its approach: World Issues World Game, Environmental Issues World Game, Cultural Awareness World Game, Ethical Issues World Game, Gender Issues World Game, Junior World Game (designed for participants in the fourth to sixth grades).

Founded in 1972, the Institute offers a variety of Fuller Projection wall maps, teacher resource guides, and many other publications, data sheets, and services. Customized programs are also available. According to Baldwin,

> The World Game Institute now has one of the largest world resource data banks in existence. (It may be *the* largest.) There are about [2,000] entries for every country. Data include such things as mineral and agricultural resources, literacy levels, human rights records, soil conditions, medical facilities, average incomes, environmental problems, and life expectancies.[80]

During recent years, the Institute has entered into strategic partnerships with the Carnegie Science Center in Pittsburgh and the Natural History Museum in New York City. These alliances touch thousands of children through outreach programs. Similar relationships with other organizations are projected.

THE ROLE OF COMPUTERS

Fuller believed that human extinction could be the price of overspecialization, but he felt that the development of the computer, the brain's "externalized adjunct,"[81] inadvertently created an "antibody" to that scenario.[82]

> We are about to have our computers take over the automation of the integrated tools that sustain you and me. Automation will take over those tools and it's going to make man utterly obsolete as a specialist. Man's going to be forced back to what he was born to be—a comprehensivist—to learn those generalized principles and to become master of his situation. This is what is coming up, if man is to make good on Earth—if we make good in time, if we catch on in time.[83]

Though some may resist the idea that everyday life will continue to become more automated, Fuller regarded technology and nature as a single, seamless circuitry—a whole. He observed,

> People worry about automation although we've all been automated ourselves. You haven't the slightest idea what you are doing this minute with your dinner; you're not purposely sending the peas and rice to this or that gland to make hair; that's all automated. You haven't the slightest idea how you went from 7 pounds to 170; it was all automated. Nobody is saying: "I'm pushing each of my hairs out in various colors and sizes"—you don't even know why you have hair. It's all automated.[84]

In a book published in 1983, well before the advent of handheld computers or the Internet as we know it, Fuller foresaw that computers would "become so miniaturized and so comprehensively capable as to be the size of a hearing aid," able to interact with other computers worldwide, and "able to discern how best to operate our planet [i.e., in the context of the World Game], making obsolete the opinions of corporate or government executives."[85]

Fuller did not believe that the world should be run by computers, but he pointed out that every time we fly in an airplane we are trusting our lives to them. As people throughout the world come to realize that future survival depends on living by holistic principles, a large computerized Geoscope—one whose simulations would be universally visible according to Fuller's original plan for the World Game—could help chart that optimum course. Simulations would be broadcast as part of the daily news via television and the Internet. Fewer errors will be made when decisions affecting the planet are based on accurate information evaluated in its holistic context rather than on shortsighted determinants such as faulty economic models, the strength of personalities, and corporate buying power.

Fuller wrote,

> I am quite confident that as the World Game is played progressively it will disclose a myriad of politically untried, unprecedented yet amazingly effective ways of solving hitherto unsurmountable world-around problems.
>
> These unprecedented computer disclosures will not only be kept track of by the computer but will become "big news" items of the world's press, and of the international news wire services. . . . The people of the world will begin to say in increasing numbers, "Now that we can see a way in which this and that can be done, as indicated by the computerized World Game, we must obviously adopt the policies indicated by the computer."[86]

DEFINITION OF WEALTH

Fuller defined wealth as consisting of two aspects. The physical component pertains to "how many forward days we have arranged for our environment to take care of us and regenerate us in life and give us increased degrees of freedom." The metaphysical component, which Fuller saw as far more important, pertains to "our intellectual capacity to recognize generalized principles that seem to be operative in the universe and to employ these principles."[87]

> That wealth combines two factors—the physical which is conserved, the metaphysical which can only increase—isn't to be found in our textbooks, but it is what we are learning. . . . There's not a single chapter in any book on economics about doing more with less. All the great secrets, how the world was run by the great powers—all

carefully omitted from the books even now. And there is still no integration of the economists with the physicists in regard to the inner significance of these matters. The economists and physicists are all too specialized. But these are the kinds of things we are going to have to learn.[88]

Fuller said that one of the "irreversibles" in the universe is that "*every* time you make an experiment you learn more; quite literally, *you cannot learn less*. . . . It means that the metaphysical factor in wealth is one that is *always* gaining."[89] He believed that "our understanding or lack of understanding of . . . what wealth really is" will directly impact the continued survival of humans on Earth.[90]

The computer will show that 70 percent of all jobs in America and probably an equivalently high percentage of the jobs in other Western private-enterprise countries are preoccupied with work that is not producing any wealth or life support—inspectors of inspectors, reunderwriters of insurance reinsurers, . . . spies and counterspies, military personnel, gunmakers, etc.[91]

Earth is the beneficiary of far more physical wealth than is generally realized.

Humanity's cosmic-energy income account consists entirely of our gravity-and-star (99 percent sun) distributed cosmic dividends of waterpower, tidal power, wavepower, windpower, vegetation-produced alcohols, methane gas, vulcanism, and so on. *Humanity's present rate of total energy consumption amounts to only one four-millionth of 1 percent of the rate of its energy income* [emphasis added].[92]

The enormity of Earth's energy income, when regarded as a whole, has profound social, economic, environmental, and educational implications:

we aboard Earth are receiving gratis
just the amount of prime energy wealth
to regenerate biological life on board,
despite our manifold ignorance,
concomitant wastage, and pollution.
That Universe tolerates our protracted nonsense
suggests significant unrealized potentials.[93]

WEAPONRY TO "LIVINGRY"

Fuller observed that "all technology is going into this great killing ring,"[94] but humans are doing very little to ensure continued life on Earth. He taught that the world's engineering and production facilities must be redirected from weaponry to "livingry."

> In contradistinction to the inherently vast wastage of World War Gaming's objectives, World Gaming takes advantage of ephemeralization—technology's ever-higher-strength-per-weight metallic alloys and chemistries and ever-more-comprehensively-incisive-and-inclusive electronic circuitry performances per volumes and weights of apparatus used—and employs ever-progressively-less weight and volume of materials, ergs of energy, and seconds of time per each technical function accomplished and employs those ever improving functions to produce ever more advanced *livingry artifacts* instead of the *killingry weapons* of World War Gaming.[95]

According to Fuller, the notion that there are too few resources for all people is no longer a valid excuse for war. From the holistic perspective, there really is enough to go around.

NATIONALISM AND POLITICS

Fuller directly addressed these two controversial subjects. At a time when there were 150 countries in the world (as distinct from 200-plus in 2001, depending on how they are counted), he stated,

> We now have 150 sovereign-state admirals simultaneously in command of our one and only Spaceship Earth. We have the starboard side of the ship trying to sink the port side, and the stern trying to secede from the rest of the ship. All the political and religious systems have demonstrated only increasing incapability to cope effectively on behalf of their side, let alone for all humanity.[96]

Fuller realized that the concepts of nationalism and patriotism have been appropriate and necessary at various times in history (during World War II, for example). Now, however, members of the human family are inextricably linked in practically every sphere of activity—business, economics, communications, the environment, travel, the arts, entertainment, foods, sports, the Internet, etc. Describing himself as "completely apolitical,"[97] Fuller felt that the appropriate governance of Spaceship Earth should exclude politics. He stated,

> I don't like politics, and I don't pay them any attention. I think that humanity has fooled itself into thinking it can do more with politics than it really can. By inventing the electric light and making it so people could work at night, Edison did more than anyone could do with politics.[98]

> We are . . . trending toward a generalized world person type, and very *rapidly*, evolutionarily speaking. You will have to realize that this is so in preparing your new educational processes in which you will have all kinds of problems arising from false fixations of society in respect to a supposedly persisting and valid nationalism, which in reality scarcely exists anywhere anymore. . . .[99]

> There is nothing in politics except knowing how to do without or taking it from one and giving it to the other. That is what the sociologists and politicians attempt to do. They still say it has to be just you *or* me. There's no real awareness among politicians anywhere around the world that there could be more-with-less to the point of making it possible for the world's available resources to take care of everybody—and at higher standards than anybody has dreamt of.[100]

Fuller went so far as to declare nationalism and politics obsolete, which may be an alarming prospect to some (possibly less so once the concept of synergy is appreciated). Although Fuller said he was not interested in politics, many of his statements make it quite clear that he really envisioned an entirely new kind of governance.

In terms of engineering, production, and logistical capability, it is possible for us to overcome the major dysfunctions that plague world society (see appendix F), but doing so will require a holistic approach. In contrast to the current system of "national boundary restrictions which 'protect' the nations,"[101] Fuller foresaw "the swift integration in a myriad of ways of all humanity not into a 'united nations' but into a united space-planet people."[102]

Comprehensive Anticipatory Design Science

Buckminster Fuller wrote,

> The success of all humanity can be accomplished only by a terrestrially comprehensive, technologically competent, design revolution. This revolution must develop artifacts whose energy-use efficiency not only occasions the artifacts' spontaneous adoption by humanity, but therewith also occasions the inadvertent, unregretted abandonment and permanent obsolescence of socially and economically undesirable viewpoints, customs, and practices.[103]

Fuller embraced diversity in all of its manifestations; his reference to "undesirable viewpoints, customs, and practices" pertains to such things as reductionist definitions of wealth and practices that "do less with more." The material in appendix F is useful in evaluating the following remarks from Fuller's *Critical Path,* which illustrate the true context of Design Science:

> From the comprehensively informed World Game viewpoint, those who have learned how to make money with money—which money can never be anything but a medium of wealth exchanging—have now completely severed money from its constant functional identity with real wealth. With their game of making money with money the money-makers and their economists continue to exploit the general and religious world's assumptions that a fundamental inadequacy of human life support exists around our planet.
>
> These money interests are wrong. Because of (A) the constant increase in strength per pound of new metallic alloys, (B) the constant increase in horsepower per each pound and cubic inch of aircraft engines, and (C) the ever-increasing performance per pounds and cubic inches of new chemistries and electronics, in general we have the capability, which can be fully realized within ten years [i.e., it would take ten years], of producing and sustaining a higher standard of living for all humanity than that ever heretofore experienced or dreamt of by any.
>
> This is not an opinion or a hope—it is an engineeringly demonstrable fact. This can be done using only the already proven technology and with the already mined, refined, and in-recirculating physical resources.
>
> This will be an inherently sustainable physical success for all humanity and all its generations to come. It can be accomplished not only within ten years [as above] but with the phasing out forever of all

use of fossil fuels and atomic energy. Our technological strategy makes it incontrovertible that we can live luxuriously entirely on our daily Sun-radiation-and-gravity-produced income energy. *The quantity of physical, cosmic energy wealth as radiation arriving aboard planet Earth each minute is greater than all the energy used annually by all humanity* [emphasis added]. World Game makes it eminently clear that we have four billion billionaires [Earth's population when Fuller wrote this] aboard our planet, as accounted by *real wealth,* which fact is obscured from public knowledge by the exclusively conceived and operated money game and its monopolized credit system accounting.[104]

These are observations that should not be lightly regarded.

Only a few of Fuller's Comprehensive Anticipatory Design Science artifacts and strategies are introduced in this chapter. A thorough study of Fuller encompasses the fields of design, engineering, geometry, shelter, construction, transportation, energy, the environment, government, economics, urban planning, and education—and includes "air-deliverable, mast-suspended dwelling machines";[105] floating cities;[106] and a three-wheeled Dymaxion car that, in 1933, could travel 120 mph (193 kph), be equipped to carry 11 passengers, and could achieve 30 miles per gallon (7.8 L/100 km).[107] Those who want to learn more might begin with Fuller's *Critical Path* or Baldwin's *BuckyWorks.*

Fuller deliberately designed far into the future "in order to avoid rousing the fears and consequent active opposition of the powerful financial, religious, and political interests who might foresee in my artifacts revolution the obsolescence of their own profitable products or services."[108] The time for the widespread use of Fuller's designs and strategies, and the holistic philosophy that inspired them, has arrived.

Intuition

Becoming a comprehensivist involves much more than mastering a prescribed holistic curriculum or methodology. The essence of comprehensivity is a *way of being*—an informed, intuitive, holistic attitude. Although Buckminster Fuller often used objective rationales in support of the holistic approach, he taught that becoming a comprehensivist ultimately relies on intuition, a topic to which he devoted an entire book.

Fuller recognized the inherent difficulty in communicating multidimensional concepts such as comprehensivity through words: "The thinking is not linear, but it has to be expressed in a linear manner; it is a matter of recording an unexpected omnidirectional involvement in a linear writing or graphing pattern."[109]

Synergetics

The mathematical expression of Fuller's holistic philosophy is known as *synergetics*. In *A Fuller Explanation,* Edmondson states that "discovering the shared principles behind structures of all materials, shapes and sizes is what synergetics is all about."[110] Fuller employed this term to identify the geometry of "nature's coordinate system," which Edmondson defines as

> the mathematically expressible system that governs the coordination of both physical and metaphysical phenomena. Set of generalizations about the way systems are structured and able to cohere over time. Interplay of the principles describing spatial complexity with the requirements of minimum energy in the organization of natural structures.[111]

Fuller said, "Synergetics represents the coming into congruence of a mathematical system integrating with the most incisive physics findings and generalized laws."[112]

> Energetic and Synergetic Geometry [i.e., synergetics] embraces all known facets of mathematics. Rather than refuting the bases of the presently known Euclidean and Non-Euclidean Hyperbolic and Elliptic geometry, Energetic-Synergetic Geometry identifies the alternative freedoms of prime axiomatic assumption from which the present mathematical bases were selected. All of the axiomatic alternatives are logical. . . . Energetic-Synergetic Geometry discovers and employs a new set of axioms which seemingly result in sublimely facile expressions of hitherto complex relationships. . . .

Energetic-Synergetic Geometry [discloses] the excruciating
awkwardness characterizing present-day mathematical treatment of
the inter-relationships of the independent scientific disciplines as
originally occasioned by their mutual and separate lacks of awareness
of the existence of a comprehensive rational coordinating system
inherent in nature.[113]

According to the author and lecturer Robert Anton Wilson,

The tensions and compressions in geodesic systems offer simpler and
more elegant formulations of our world than either the traditional
Euclidean-Aristotelian-Newtonian systems or the "revised" modern
systems which still use pre-Fullerian geometries.

All the paradoxes and mind-boggling Strange Loops that infest
"modern" (post-quantum) science now appear, in Fuller's recounting,
as the results of applying Descartes' algebration of Euclid's flat-land
geometry to a spherical space where Euclid just does not work. In
Fuller's geometry, the paradoxes and Strange Loops simply do not
occur. Universe becomes astoundingly "rational" again.[114]

Edmondson writes,

Synergetics, in the broadest terms, is the study of spatial complexity,
and as such is an inherently comprehensive discipline. Designers,
architects, and scientists can easily find applications of this study in
their work; however, the larger significance of Fuller's geometry may
be less visible. Experience with synergetics encourages a new way of
approaching and solving problems. Its emphasis on visual and spatial
phenomena combined with Fuller's holistic approach fosters the kind
of lateral thinking which so often leads to creative breakthroughs.[115]

Among all his inventions and discoveries, Fuller considered
synergetics to have the greatest potential as a force for ensuring
humanity's success.[116] Those interested in architecture, design, topog-
raphy, geometry, sacred geometry, and human evolution will find a
veritable treasure within this subject.

Misconditioned Reflexes[117]

Fuller taught that becoming educated comprehensively is the only
way to overcome our obsolete conditioning. For example, he pointed
out the error in referring to astronauts as going "up" into space and
then coming back "down" to Earth. Words like "up" and "down,"

Fuller said, were invented to explain what seemed to be happening in a world that appeared flat. "But the earth is spherical—and none of the perpendiculars are, of course, parallel to one another. What may be up at one point is not necessarily up to another point."[118]

For five centuries, people have known that the sun, rather than coming up or going down, is revealed or obscured by Earth's revolutions. Therefore, Fuller used the terms "sunsight" and "sunclipse."[119] Although the words sunrise and sunset are replete with poetic imagery, Fuller pointed out that words can create erroneous reflexes that skew our perception of reality. He said,

> All humanity's reflexing is as yet so ill-conditioned by years of optical illusion, self-deception and general-education-dispensed misinformation, that it goes right on coddling its own ignorance as well as overwhelming its children with the inventory of formally tolerated errors, thus perpetuating and increasing the polluted information.[120]

On Spaceship Earth, the words "up" and "down" have no absolute meaning; therefore, there is no upstairs and downstairs. Going "outstairs" and "instairs"—away from and towards the center of the planet—is what occurs.[121] Wind doesn't blow, it is sucked (air being sucked into a low-pressure zone from a zone of higher pressure causes the wind to "blow"). It might seem nonsensical to stress these points of usage in everyday conversation; however, if our perceptions were based on what is actually occurring in the natural world, perhaps this would influence our actions in areas such as consumption habits, economic policies, and the environment, leading to effective solutions.

Mathematical concepts can also condition perceptions. Fuller said that experiments have "invalidated most mathematics axioms *still* being taught in schools everywhere."[122] For example, it is impossible to find a straight line extending into space for the simple reason that Earth revolves around its own axis at approximately 1,000 miles per hour (1,609 kph) while orbiting the sun at approximately 67,000 miles an hour (108,000 kph). Perceived comprehensively, a line could never be really straight; it would be like a spiral or corkscrew.[123]

Everything you've learned in school as "obvious" becomes less and less obvious as you begin to study the universe. For example, there are no solids in the universe. There's not even a suggestion of a solid. There are no absolute continuums. There are no surfaces. There are no straight lines.[124]

[Teachers] say, "I'm going to give you *plane* geometry," not even cubical geometry. So you have to pretend there's something called a "plane," even though you can't have a surface by itself—it has to be the surface of something. And anything that has a surface must also have an *insideness* and an *outsideness*.

So you might as well start with reality, and not with the fake imaginary plane that doesn't even exist.[125]

Fuller believed that education should reflect the way things really are in the natural world where objects have mass, temperature, duration, and relationship.

Around the world nothing has ever been formally instituted in our educational systems to gear the human senses into spontaneous accord with our scientific knowledge. In fact, much has been done and much has been left undone by powerful world institutions that prevents such reorientation of our misconditioned reflexes. Our own misconditioned reflexes are powerful deterrents to our successful self-reorientation of our apprehending faculties to accord with the emerging truths.[126]

In light of the global environmental crisis, continuing to perceive the world through misconditioned reflexes is not a viable option.

Invisible Reality

Buckminster Fuller taught that reality is not what we have always considered it to be:

Up to the twentieth century, "reality" was everything humans could touch, smell, see, and hear. Since the initial publication of the chart of the electromagnetic spectrum in 1930, humans have learned that what they can touch, smell, see, and hear is less than one-millionth of reality. Ninety-nine percent of all that is going to affect our tomorrows is being developed by humans using instruments and working in the ranges of reality that are non-humanly sensible.[127]

Readers who desire a thorough exploration of Fuller's thinking with regard to the invisible realm might begin with his book *Cosmography*. Published posthumously in 1992, this book outlines what he considered to be the twelve most extraordinary cases of the human mind's ability to discover invisible interrelationships, including Democritus' conception of atoms, Lavoisier's conception of the "differentiation of the undifferentiated nothingness into identifiable gases," and Hertz's discovery of electromagnetic waves.[128]

Invisible interrelationships also pertain to the environmental situation. In the past, human survival depended on the ability to react to visible, tangible threats (a hungry carnivore, a rampaging elephant). Today our survival depends on learning to perceive and react to threats that are principally *un*seen, such as biodiversity loss and ozone depletion.

The Role of Education

"Education for comprehensivity" concisely summarizes Fuller's view about the role of education. "Every child is born a genius," he said, but "99 percent are degeniused by early post-natal circumstances."[129] He pointed out that children are born comprehensive and want "to understand the whole thing . . . Universe." [130]

If one purpose of educational inquiry is to improve the well-being of humanity, it follows that the relative viability of humanity (and its environment) is an appropriate yardstick for measuring the quality of education.[131] Indeed, Fuller held the education system accountable for many of our social and environmental problems. He believed that the world's education systems have conditioned people to "linear special-case-directions thinking," and this "despite all experiencing being inherently omnidirectionally informed."[132]

> We have coddled our "realists'" retention of the thought habit of Earth as the immovable center of the Universe. We have coddled the scientifically untenable concepts of matter as static "things." We speak of the chemical elements as materials. We think of "metals" as

static absolutes rather than as subvisible dynamic systems. We have vacillated in adjusting our practical thinking to synchronization with the infinite motion of systematic processes of the all-dynamic Universe in which we must survive. The viewpoint of scholastic administration and lay intelligence has alike been static despite its dynamic intentions and promises.[133]

Fuller recognized the depth of society's fixation on reductionist thinking and behavior:

It is readily understandable why humans, born utterly helpless, utterly ignorant, have been prone to cope in an elementary way with successive experiences or "parts." They are so overwhelmed by the synergetic mystery of the whole as to have eschewed educational strategies commencing with Universe and the identification of the separate experiences within the cosmic totality.[134]

Fortunately, Fuller and others have made holistic strategies available and easy to learn.

Because most formal education systems have been slow to recognize the holistic paradigm, self-education is the primary vehicle through which individuals become comprehensivists. Self-education may incorporate relevant classroom learning activities, but it also entails such life-long endeavors as independently reading, listening to audiotapes, watching videos, undertaking research projects, constructing physical models, going on field trips, and taking on apprenticeships.[135]

THE USE OF COMPUTERS

In addition to the use of computers in World Game simulations, Buckminster Fuller had much to say about their role in day-to-day education. Although schools have essential functions, which include the imparting of necessary social skills, Fuller felt that education must also take place in the home. Ideally, each child would have a private area containing educational aids such as dictionaries and maps, as well as an "individually selected and articulated two-way TV and an intercontinentally networked, documentaries call-up system, operative over any home two-way TV set."[136]

As early as 1932, Fuller envisioned "instant call-up of data" for use in problem solving and decision making.[137] In a 1962 essay he predicted that graduate students and faculty, assisted by instructional technologists and communications specialists, would one day create feature-length video documentaries in their areas of expertise. The videos would become available in a great library of human knowledge accessed through the "two-way TV" he described. Videos would be periodically re-edited and updated so that the *net* knowledge of any subject would be available.[138] With the advent of interactive CD-ROMs and the Internet, some aspects of Fuller's vision for education have become realities. "Education for comprehensivity" is the next step.

Of course, there are downsides to the impact of computers on society.[139] Time spent at computers cannot replace learning through experience in the real world. A holistic approach advocates balance. Fuller understood that direct contact with inspirational teachers is vital in helping students to shape their lives. Yet holistically oriented educational software of high quality and contact with teachers primarily by way of computer may be more effective than classes taught in person by uninspired or complacent teachers invested in outmoded ways of thinking.

MODELABILITY[140]

Models were basic to Fuller's teaching method, and he taught that physically modeling key concepts should be an integral component of education. Modeling helps us learn about relationships in nature through personal discovery.

Simulations available with the Geoscope and the World Game are only one type of modeling. Fuller also encouraged working with three-dimensional geometric models in learning about synergetics and generalized principles.[141] The antithesis of over-intellectualizing, modeling enables the potentially complex phenomena of synergetics to be easily understood, even by young students.

Once while conversing with the English physicist and novelist C. P. Snow (1905-1980), Fuller disagreed with Snow about the reason for the gap between the "two cultures," the sciences and the humanities. According to one account of their conversation, Fuller

> did not agree that this gap had been caused by a spontaneous aversion to industrialization on the part of literary men. In Fuller's opinion, scientists had caused it. Soon after the discovery of electromagnetics, in the nineteenth century, he said, scientists had decided that because electrical energy was invisible, it could not be represented to the layman in the form of models, and so they had decided to stop trying to explain what they were doing in terms that the layman could understand. "That's really the great myth of the nineteenth century," he said. "I told Snow the basic reason for the split was that science gave up models."[142]

Synergetics enables invisible generalized principles and nature's structural relationships to be modeled—an activity that could contribute to the reunification of the sciences and the humanities.

FULLER AND MONTESSORI

There are many similarities between Fuller's holistic philosophy and that of the famed educator Maria Montessori (1870-1952).[143] Fuller admired the Montessori System's "education by choice,"[144] wherein children explore subjects they are naturally drawn to and learn at their own pace. Both taught that a child's spontaneously expanding nature should not be tampered with, and that a properly prepared educational environment is essential. The use of specific educational artifacts is central to both educators' methods. They saw that interacting with these sensory objects (in Fuller's case, geometric models) leads children to discover universal principles on their own. In Montessori's words, "The important thing is to give a cosmic idea, one complete whole, the universe, for the child's mind . . . seeks not only facts but their underlying causes, and you cannot properly see the connections until you have first seen the whole."[145]

THE INTERSECTION OF SCIENCE AND ART

Fuller encouraged people to become comprehensive design scientists in the fullest sense—architects of their universe. To him, science was an art form in which nature and technology met. Due to their ability to formulate conceptually, he considered artists to be innate comprehensivists. They keep modelability alive, and their work is generally intuitive, often a reflection of many disciplines. Indeed, artists have always modeled elements of the invisible realm, turning their personal visions into material creations.

In the tradition of Leonardo da Vinci, one of Buckminster Fuller's most intriguing traits was that he combined the sensibilities of scientist and artist. As has been shown, he presented some of his technical ideas in the form of prose poems. He counted among his friends many artists of all kinds, including Thornton Wilder, Christopher Morley, Salvador Dali, Ezra Pound, John Cage, Martha Graham, Katherine Dunham, Jasper Johns, Marshall McLuhan, Merce Cunningham, Willem de Kooning, Frank Lloyd Wright, Robert Rauschenberg, Isamu Noguchi, Arthur C. Clarke, John Denver, Norman Cousins, John Huston, Annie Dillard, and Isaac Asimov.

MISTAKE MYSTIQUE

Fuller presented some of his ideas about teachers' evaluations of students in an essay titled "Mistake Mystique."[146] He stated that much can be learned not only through the process of producing correct answers, but through a close personal examination of one's errors:

> At present, teachers, professors, and their helpers go over the students' examinations, looking for errors. They usually ratio the percentage of error to the percentage of correctly remembered concepts to which the students have been exposed. I suggest that the teaching world alter this practice and adopt the requirement that all students periodically submit a written account of all the mistakes they have made, not only regarding the course subject, but in their self-discipline during the term, while also recording what they have learned

from the recognition that they have made the mistakes; the reports should summarize what it is they have really learned, not only in their courses, but on their own intuition and initiative. I suggest, then, that the faculty be marked as well as the students on a basis of their effectiveness in helping the students to learn anything important about any subject—doing so by nature's prescribed trial and error leverage. The more mistakes the students discover, the higher their grade.[147]

Integrity

Fuller was once asked, "What do you think is the greatest challenge facing young people today as they prepare to assume their caretakership of this world?"[148] He answered,

> From my viewpoint, by far the greatest challenge facing the young people today is that of responding and conforming only to their own most delicately insistent intuitive awarenesses of what the truth seems to them to be as based on their own experiences and not on what others have interpreted to be the truth regarding events of which neither they nor others have experience-based knowledge.
>
> This also means not yielding unthinkingly to "in" movements or to crowd psychology. This involves assessing thoughtfully one's own urges. It involves understanding but not being swayed by the spontaneous group spirit of youth. It involves thinking before acting in every instance. It involves eschewing all loyalties to other than the truth and love through which the cosmic integrity and absolute wisdom we identify inadequately by the name "God" speaks to each of us directly—and speaks only through our individual awareness of truth and our most spontaneous and powerful emotions of love and compassion.[149]

During the last years of his life, Fuller said that integrity was at the core of all he had been able to accomplish and was central to his teaching.

> [He valued] the *power of personal integrity* as a force in the world, available to each of us, that transcends our "position" in life, our particular abilities and skills, and the specific circumstances in which we find ourselves. He saw this power of personal integrity as a force capable of steering humanity towards the realization of a world that truly works for everybody.[150]

Fuller stressed that more people must learn to apply holistic principles if we are to reverse the trends that jeopardize the survival of our species. To Fuller, personal integrity called for "the courage to adhere to the truth as we learn it."[151] He stated, "I think this particular Earthian colonization is in a final examination to see whether we humans have the intellectual integrity to go with our minds or are we going to go with our crowd psychology brains."[152] He elaborated:

> The present evolutionary crisis of humans on planet Earth is that of a final examination for their continuance in Universe. It is not an examination of political, economic, or religious systems, but of the integrity of each and all individual humans' responsible thinking and unselfish response to the acceleration in evolution's ever more unprecedented events.[153]

Fuller believed that we would ultimately be successful in overcoming our "crowd psychology brains," but he knew that doing so would not be easy.

> At the very moment humanity has arrived at that evolutionary point where we do have the option for everyone to "make it," I find it startling to discover that all the great governments, the five great religions, and most of big business would find it absolutely devastating to their continuance to have humanity become a physical, metabolic, economic success. All the political, religious, and money-making institutions' power is built upon those institutions' expertise in ministering to, and ameliorating, the suffering, want, pain, and fears resultant upon the misassumption of a fundamental inadequacy of life support on our planet and the consequent misfortune of the majority of humans.[154]

Courage is required in order to change. Integrity is the interface between conceiving a viable philosophy of life and each day living it.

Response to Criticisms of Fuller

Various criticisms of Buckminster Fuller have emerged over the years, yet he needs defending no more than a toolbox needs defending. He has provided a set of holistic tools designed to help humans achieve success in the universe. However, some have called his ideas overly complicated or too technological, and his language "mechanistic." For example, critics have asserted that equating Earth, a geo-biosphere, with a spaceship suggests a sterile, inorganic machine.

Fuller's work concerns the whole, so his various artifacts and strategies should not be criticized in isolation. Examining the concept of Spaceship Earth a bit further will reveal the importance of evaluating his work in its holistic context. To those who have not studied Fuller's strategies in depth, the term Spaceship Earth may indeed appear somewhat mechanistic. This analogy, however, skillfully illustrates possibilities not encompassed by conceiving Earth as a biosphere (a perspective that has its own unique advantages).

Fuller used the term Spaceship Earth as a visual, relational teaching tool. Although he recognized syntropy and our dependence on the "energy-supplying mothership," the sun,[155] he knew that Earth is in some respects a closed system with finite resources. "Spaceship Earth" accurately and rather poetically conveys this notion. Humans, in our attempts to dominate the rest of nature, have to some extent placed ourselves "in control" of this ship. Now, we must act in ways that will allow and assist the rest of nature, which happens to be Earth's human life-support system, to recover and rebalance.

The biosphere model would seem to imply that everything that needs to happen in nature will just unfold organically (which is true); however, humans, in our efforts to take control of nature, have speeded things up. The evolutionary changes that will have to occur, in order to remedy the environmental destruction we have wrought in the past 100 years and continue to inflict, will have to come from within humanity itself.

Photovoltaic panels don't spring forth from the ground ready to use. It is incumbent on humans to take the holistic actions necessary on a spaceship that is steadily losing its integrity. In this context, having an "Operating Manual for Spaceship Earth" (the title of one of Fuller's books, noted in appendix B) seems like an excellent idea.

Perhaps the spaceship concept will make it easier for people to see that those in one compartment of the "ship" are interdependent with those in the other compartments—before the fires in the galleys rage out of control. The Spaceship Earth metaphor is one more way to help us *see what is,* in order to get people to think about and take action regarding our predicament.

Furthermore, the Spaceship Earth map (the Fuller Projection) is the ideal tool for playing the World Game so that we can evaluate the various options and strategies available to us. The two models, Spaceship Earth and biosphere-Earth, are not mutually exclusive. Who is to say that a spaceship can't be a living biosphere? Criticisms of Fuller should not be based on his choice of terminology. The ramifications of his teachings far outweigh such commentary.

Fuller has also been criticized for placing too much emphasis on design and technology for solving the problems of humanity; this has been interpreted as his own brand of reductionism. Technology has become associated (for good reason) with environmental degradation and dehumanization. Distinctions must be made, however, between Fuller's technological inventions (which are often described in the language of an engineer) and the underlying holistic, humanitarian philosophy that inspired them. Applewhite notes, "[Fuller's] philosophy was never a rationale for the domes, rather the domes were an attempt to explain his philosophy."[156]

It is helpful to view Fuller in the context of his time. The formative years of his late teens and early twenties occurred during World War I when engineers and inventors were considered among society's true heroes. Despite reductionist patterns of industrialization that were intensifying around him, Fuller became a modern pioneer in the fields of applied holism, holistic education, and ecology.

While Fuller employed the nomenclature of an engineer, he had the soul of a poet. To him, technology *was* biology (i.e., an outgrowth of it). He knew the genius reflected in nature to be vastly superior to human intelligence, believing that as investigators discovered more about nature, technological designs would correspondingly improve.[157] Fuller would never consider dismantling nature in order to sell it part by part, nor did he try to improve upon it in the laboratory. Instead, his artifacts embody and take advantage of nature's mathematics and design principles. Fuller's technological artifacts and ecological views are much better aligned with the holistic subtleties of nature than his critics seem to realize.[158]

Fuller encouraged a holistic design science revolution. Computers and other high technology devices could play a crucial role in addressing complex global, regional, and local problems brought on by adherence to unsustainable production and consumption practices. Although technology can be employed constructively, many of its by-products and side effects are inherently harmful. Buckminster Fuller's philosophy addresses how to use technology without disadvantaging life forms and the physical environment. Therefore, rather than discounting his philosophy as "too technological" or "not organic enough," it should be welcomed and studied deeply.

Some of Fuller's concerns about the future have been criticized as apocalyptic. But in light of pronouncements by the Union of Concerned Scientists and the Intergovernmental Panel on Climate Change, it appears that his predictions could materialize unless world leaders and people everywhere develop a holistic outlook. While many educators and philosophers may only theorize about or lament conditions, Fuller took action by developing tangible solutions to help us evolve holistically.

Fuller's work was challenging to some critics because he worked from the whole, not inductively from within any particular context, but comprehensively using intuitive insight. Some have said, in effect, that his work appears disconnected, that it doesn't build on previous knowledge, and that he is trying to reinvent the wheel and rediscover Einstein all at once. But Fuller *did* invent a "new wheel"—

energetic-synergetic geometry (synergetics)—and his discovery of unique, practical applications of Einstein's work was acknowledged by Einstein himself.[159]

As noted earlier, Buckminster Fuller's work always pertains to the whole; therefore, it can legitimately be evaluated only by its contribution to the body of knowledge regarding the whole.

To Learn More

This overview of R. Buckminster Fuller outlines the basics of his philosophy. Those who are interested in learning more have many means of doing so. In addition to the numerous books he wrote and presentations he recorded on audiotape and video, more than fifteen books have been written about him and his contributions. He has been the subject of several documentaries and hundreds of articles, including a 1964 *Time* magazine cover story.[160]

Among the books by or about Fuller are those emphasizing different facets of his work (architecture, design, engineering, synergetics, education, etc.) and those specifically written for children, as well as autobiographical works and biographies.

The full scope of Fuller's thinking is revealed in his 1981 book, *Critical Path.* It may be better understood and appreciated, however, by first reading Baldwin's *BuckyWorks,* published in 1996. This clear and comprehensive book contains many photos and other illustrations, a selected bibliography, and a list of resources. Baldwin worked with Fuller for more than thirty years and served as an editor of the *Whole Earth Catalog* and the *Whole Earth Review* for twenty-five years. Of Fuller's book *Critical Path,* Baldwin writes:

> This is Bucky's most complete presentation of what we must do (soon) to make our species the success it can be. The major points of his earlier works are united into a grand strategy for education and action—truly a recipe for life. It's the best review of his comprehensive thinking, and a lot easier to digest than *Synergetics.* The undertone of urgency is contagious. If you're going to read just one book by Bucky, this is it.[161]

Reading *BuckyWorks* and *Critical Path* will help one decide which aspects of Fuller's work to explore in greater detail. Edmondson's book, *A Fuller Explanation,* is invaluable for those who want to know more about synergetics but who may initially balk at entering the philosophical and highly technical world of *Synergetics: Explorations in the Geometry of Thinking* or *Synergetics 2: Further Explorations in the Geometry of Thinking.*[162] Another doorway to synergetic geometry is *Fuller's Earth: A Day with Bucky and the Kids,* by Richard J. Brenneman.[163] Fuller is quoted at length in this book, making synergetics and other seemingly complex subjects intelligible to children aged ten and over. Brenneman's book is also an excellent introduction to synergetics for adults.

Books by or about Buckminster Fuller are available in libraries, through the Interlibrary Loan System, through the Buckminster Fuller Institute, and in used/out-of-print book stores (including those on the Web). Spiral-bound photocopy versions of some out-of-print books are available through the Institute.

BUCKMINSTER FULLER INSTITUTE

Located in Sebastopol, California, this nonprofit educational organization serves as a resource center for students, educators, authors, designers, and others. Its mission is to "catalyze awareness and action towards realizing humanity's option for success."[164] The Institute offers educational materials and networking assistance "concerning projects, events, and individual initiatives to people interested in addressing human trends and needs," as well as courses in design science.[165] Through its Dymaxion Catalog (available by mail or on their Web site; see appendix C), the Institute also provides books, maps, audio/video recordings, models, and toys. The Web site features material from the Fuller Archives and the complete text of several of his most popular books. A site map is provided for navigating this record of Fuller's universe. In addition to the Institute's Web site, there are hundreds of sites that celebrate his work. The Fuller Archives were acquired in 1999 by the Department of Special Collections, Stanford University Libraries.[166]

Fuller's Legacy

Buckminster Fuller occupies a unique position among the modern pioneers of holism. Numerous holistically oriented authors and practitioners credit him as one of their major teachers. The totality of his work serves as an inspiration and guide for thinking and performing comprehensively.

Fuller may well have been one of the greatest educators of all time. The American poet, dramatist, and critic Archibald MacLeish (1892-1982) observed, "If any man's life has reconciled our early spiritual achievements with our later scientific triumphs, it is [Fuller's]."[167] Although the artifacts and strategies for success are of

tremendous importance, some of his greatest contributions occur on another level. According to Applewhite, Fuller's primary vocation was that of poet:

> All his disciplines and talents—architect, engineer, philosopher, inventor, artist, cartographer, teacher—are just so many aspects of his chief function as integrator. When [Fuller] was appointed to the Charles Eliot Norton chair of poetry at Harvard in 1962, he described the word "poet" as a very general term for a person who puts things together in an era of great specialization when most people are differentiating or taking things apart. . . . For Fuller, the stuff of poetry is the patterns of human behavior and the environment, and the interacting hierarchies of physics and design and industry.[168]

The noted literary critic Hugh Kenner has written that Fuller gave us a "system of coherencies . . . for our space age navigating." Kenner stated, "The crisis to which synergetics is pertinent is a crisis of popular enlightenment, popular faith. . . . Metaphors, paradigms, these are our deepest needs."[169]

Fuller provided a vision of our potential success as voyagers on Spaceship Earth. His views on planetary well-being and self-discovery are distilled in his statement, *"To be optimally effective, undertake at outset the most comprehensive task in the most comprehensive and incisively detailed manner."* When this single principle is put into general practice, humanity will make great progress, synergistically.

One of Fuller's colleagues summarized,

> The impact [Fuller] had was to help people understand that larger wholes really matter. Spaceship Earth [is] that larger perspective that gives people a context. . . . Many people throughout history have talked about such things. But Bucky was different—he was the first person who made a "world view" and a "science" out of starting with the whole, with Universe. Nobody did that as comprehensively and as honestly as he did.[170]

When developing his artifacts and strategies, Fuller designed fifty years into the future so that when more people were ready to appreciate the value of comprehensive solutions, many of these solutions would already be available.

Humans are coming swiftly to understand they must now con-
sciously begin to operate their space vehicle Earth with total
planetary cooperation, competence, and integrity. Humans are
swiftly sensing that the cushioning tolerance for their initial error has
become approximately exhausted.[171]

I am certain that none of the world's problems—which we are all
perforce thinking about today—have any hope of solution except
through total democratic society's becoming thoroughly and comprehensively self-educated. Only thereby will society be able to
identify and intercommunicate the vital problems of total world
society. Only thereafter may humanity effectively sort out and put
those problems into order of importance for solution in respect to the
most fundamental principles governing humanity's survival and
enjoyment of life on Earth.[172]

Your educational forces, if competently organized and instru-
mented, should stimulate the self clean-up. The politicians won't
clean up; the only hope is through education.[173]

Because he knew that genuine education requires a universal outlook, Buckminster Fuller did not limit his discussion to physical
reality but referred frequently to the metaphysical realm. In any
field, an approach that disregards this realm is actually reductionist, focusing only on parts of the whole. Next we explore Tao, a term
originated by ancient Chinese sages to convey that which cannot be
conveyed through words.

CHAPTER 3

Tao

Great knowledge sees all in one.
Small knowledge breaks down into the many.

CHUANG-TZU

"The Inexpressible"

Tao pops up all over the place. What does this mean, and what does it have to do with wholeness? One can find hundreds of books with *Tao* (usually pronounced "dow") as part of the title. In this book, *Tao* is used as a convenient word to indicate "the inexpressible." In attempting a definition, *The Encyclopedia of Eastern Philosophy and Religion* states that the term is actually undefinable.

Tao Chin., lit. "Way"; central concept of Taoism . . . and origin of its name. . . .

Although the original meaning of the pictogram for Tao is "Way," it can also denote "Teaching." . . . The *Tao-te ching* of Lao-tzu is the first text to ascribe a metaphysical meaning to the term, in the sense that it is seen as the all-embracing first principle, from which all appearances arise. It is a reality that gives rise to the universe. Lao-tzu referred to it as the Tao only because there was no other adequate term available. In the translation of Chang Chung-yuan (1963):

> There was something complete and nebulous
> Which existed before the Heaven and Earth,
> Silent, invisible,
> Unchanging, standing as One,
> Unceasing, ever-revolving,
> Able to be the Mother of the World.
> I do not know its name and call it Tao.

The Tao then is nameless, unnamable. . . .[1]

This chapter is not concerned with what the Taoist scholar, poet, and Trappist monk Thomas Merton (1915-1968) termed "the popular, degenerate amalgam of superstition, alchemy, magic, and health-culture which Taoism later became,"[2] or its reinvention and transformation into a popularized religion.[3] Instead, we will investigate the philosophy of wholeness embodied in the words of Lao-tzu (fl. sixth century B.C.E.)[4] and Chuang-tzu (fl. fourth century B.C.E.). This philosophy is not a religion, but it does include concepts that could be described as transcendent.[5] A person of Tao might not use this term at all, affirming that ordinary reality is transcendent and the transcendent is ordinary. When everything is sacred, there is no need to single out anything. No wonder ancient masters taught that Tao could not be grasped intellectually. Chuang-tzu said,

> To name Tao
> Is to name no-thing.
> Tao is not the name
> Of "an existent."
> "Cause" and "chance"
> Have no bearing on Tao.
> Tao is a name
> That indicates
> Without defining.
>
> Tao is beyond words
> And beyond things.
> It is not expressed
> Either in word or in silence.
> Where there is no longer word or silence
> Tao is apprehended.[6]

Apprehension of Tao implies unity, balance, living in tune with the whole—which includes the apparent dualities and vicissitudes of everyday life. Individually and as a society, we have generally become immersed in duality while remaining blind to the whole.

Tao, the Absolute, the One Mind,[7] Integral Oneness, Holy Spirit, Great Mother, Divine Principle—whatever the label, Tao is beyond words. Still, the ancient sages taught that a human's birthright—one's ordinary, essential nature—is to realize the oneness of all being, to exist and act in that state of wholeness.

Spirituality

Spirituality is intrinsic to the holistic approach, and holistic education embraces the spiritual dimension—the archetypal, transpersonal, cosmic dimension of being.[8] Rather than adhering to a single belief system or denomination, wholeness encompasses and honors all religions and beliefs.

At present, in much of the world, it is difficult to explicitly acknowledge spirit in public education systems. Using such terms as spirit and Tao could evoke charges that the state is promulgating religion. But the charges would be incorrect. The difference between spirituality and religion is clearly expressed by James Moffett (1929-1996), educator and author of *The Universal Schoolhouse: Spiritual Awakening through Education.*

> Even in its most sacred sense, spirituality does not depend on religion. Spirituality may be what all religions share, but religions are human-made and partake of particular cultures, so much so that their adherents may confuse Spirit with race spirit and continually slaughter each other over cultural differences construed as conflicts between the holy and unholy.[9]

> *Spiritual* does not mean pollyanna, puritanical, or pietistic. Nor does it refer to a sect or even to religion in general, inasmuch as all religions are embodied in cultural institutions that are partial. Spirituality is totally cosmopolitan, because only the cosmic framework is all-inclusive. To be spiritual is to perceive our oneness with everybody and everything and to act on this perception. It is to be whole within oneself and with the world. Morality ensues. From this feeling of unity proceed all positive things, just as from *whole* proceed all the words for these things—*wholesome, hale, healthy,* and *holy.*

> A society can become sacred through secular means. Spiritualizing education does not require any religious indoctrination or moralistic preaching. All it takes is the setting of certain relationships among people and between people and the rest of nature.[10]

The Perennial Philosophy

Throughout human history, mystics, sages, and philosophers have identified a common core, a golden thread running through all spiritual traditions. In the opening words of *The Perennial Philosophy*, English novelist and essayist Aldous Huxley (1894-1963) wrote:

> Philosophia Perennis—the phrase was coined by Leibniz [Gottfried Wilhelm von Leibniz (1646-1716), German philosopher, writer, and mathematician]; but the thing—the metaphysic that recognizes a divine Reality substantial to the world of things and lives and minds; the psychology that finds in the soul something similar to, or even identical with, divine Reality; the ethic that places man's final end in the knowledge of the immanent and transcendent Ground of all being—the thing is immemorial and universal. . . . A version of this Highest Common Factor in all . . . theologies . . . has been treated again and again, from the standpoint of every religious tradition. . . .
>
> The nature of this one Reality is such that it cannot be directly and immediately apprehended except by those who have chosen to fulfill certain conditions, making themselves loving, pure in heart, and poor in spirit.[11]

Considering our limited knowledge of how we and the world are put together, there is ample reason for us to be spiritually humble.

Wonderment

Despite great achievements in art, science, and medicine, we remain ignorant about the basic elements of existence. Scientists and engineers build incredible spacecraft that fly to distant planets and "smart" bombs that destroy by remote control. But how much is really known about life itself? We know that we are here, we can procreate, and we have even mapped the human genome. However, many aspects of life remain a mystery.

We live in a solar system that is not of our own creation. We do not know how to make a rain forest, yet they nurture much of the life on the planet. Humans have uncovered the wonder of photosyn-thesis, but we have never duplicated it. Our amazingly intricate bodies develop without any conscious direction from us. We did not create flowers, but they are everywhere in endless color and variety. We cannot create a mango (from scratch), let alone a flamingo.

Yet, everything is here. Isn't the presence of life in all of its mani-festations—on a planet functioning in a coherent fashion in an organized solar system in what is said to be an ever-expanding uni-verse[12]—cause enough for reverence? Our mere existence is proof of the unfathomable mysteries of the whole. Have any human accom-plishments truly improved upon the operating system that created life and the natural world? With holistic awareness comes a hum-bling recognition of the immeasurable intelligence at play within all creation—an intelligence that has produced and continues to produce a universe more complex and fantastic than anyone could devise, much less construct.[13]

Throughout the ages, masters have taught that every person can experience the whole because all beings are of this selfsame whole. To encounter its mysteries requires only a state of simple presence and quietude. Nature (including human nature) is the great holistic teacher. Nothing surpasses the artistry, inventiveness, and diversity of nature—an experience of unnamable, immeasurable Tao.

Waterfalls, roses, birds, love, sunshine, trees, spiders, straw-berries. Space. What a marvelous existence! Friendship, spaghetti, elephants! Our wondrous bodies and minds. When one pauses to consider it all, the totality is astonishing. The energies associated with the direct experience of wholeness are transformative.

Compassion

Recognizing our personal connection with the whole brings with it the understanding that the potential for this same recognition exists in everyone. We begin to appreciate wholeness in every person.

Attitudes spontaneously shift from exclusionary to inclusionary, from exploitative to nurturing, from manipulative to supportive, from self-absorbed to caring, from despondent to joyous, from superior to modest and accepting. In essence, this shift reflects a profound compassion and respect for all life.

Therefore, "the whole" has a signature. The "test" for holism is its fruitage. Is a particular person, group, or action supportive of life processes? Inclusive? Non-exploitative? Loving? Purported holism—without sensitivity, tenderness, compassion, and love—is a hoax.

It is simplistic to hypothesize that when people experience oneness, everything will be perfect in the world, since there is still the ongoing challenge of integrating wholeness into daily life. But those who discover oneness do exhibit compassion for all existence.

When Tao Is Denied

DISCONNECTION

Reductionist, overspecialized education, information overload, and a host of other social, psychological, and economic factors have led to a society that is disconnected from wholeness. Bombarded on all sides by "communication," real connection that is fundamentally honest, open, and forthright is often hard to find. Disconnectedness is exacerbated by the mass media, especially television and movies, which feature endless themes of violence, greed, murder, manipulation, deception, and domination. The fact that such behavior exists in "real life" is no excuse for its relentless reinforcement. At the same time, our desires for connection, certainty, and fulfillment are constantly stimulated by advertisements that combine state-of-the-art consumer psychology with sophisticated and seductive production techniques.

This milieu of disconnectedness has enormous social and psychological consequences. The philosopher and author Ivan Illich expressed the situation well: "So pervasive is the power of the institutions we have created that they shape not only our preferences, but actually our sense of possibilities."[14] The theoretical physicist David Bohm (1917-1992) suggested an alternative:

> Man's general way of thinking of the totality, i.e., his general world view, is crucial for overall order of the human mind itself. If he thinks of the totality as constituted of independent fragments, then that is how his mind will tend to operate, but if he can include everything coherently and harmoniously in an overall whole that is undivided, unbroken, and without border (for every border is a division or break) then his mind will tend to move in a similar way, and from this will flow an orderly action within the whole.
>
> Of course . . . our general world view is not the *only* factor that is important in this context. Attention must, indeed, be given to many other factors, such as emotions, physical activities, human relationships, social organizations, etc., but perhaps because we have at present no coherent world view, there is a widespread tendency to ignore the psychological and social importance of such questions almost altogether. My suggestion is that a proper world view, appropriate for its time, is generally one of the basic factors that is essential for harmony in the individual and in society as a whole.[15]

As we learn about and experience wholeness we develop a coherent world view, expanding our sense of what is possible.

SKEWED PERCEPTION OF REALITY

Awakening to wholeness enhances a person's ability to perceive what is. Those who ignore the reality of the whole either lack education on the "subject" or, for whatever reason, refuse to allow it. At this time, we are in dire need of educational approaches that are in tune with holistic realities. A central aspect of Tao in practice calls for action in accordance with the natural flow of events, action that is appropriate to a given situation and based on an unclouded perspective.

FUNDAMENTALISM

Fundamentalism appears in many forms: religious, racial, political, economic, philosophical, sociological, educational, scientific. Fundamentalists "know" that their individual religion, philosophy, nation, organization, or tribe is sanctified above all others. They are fixated on one part, insisting that it is the whole. A well-known manifestation takes the form "My God is better than your God." In the extreme, fundamentalists think that people who believe differently should be eliminated. Since fundamentalism is the result of mental conditioning, wholeness is the desired focus in psychological/spiritual counseling.

"SPIRITUAL-PECKING-ORDER-ITIS"

Fundamentalism occurs in varying degrees, even among holistic, spiritual, shamanistic, and "new age" personalities. It is ironic that "spiritual-pecking-order-itis" can be observed in groups where wholeness is the professed theme. Tao is not about whose form of meditation, yoga, or medicine is best, debating the fine points of intellectual constructs, or expressing them in perfect Sanskrit. It has been said that the paths of teachers and healers can be especially difficult because they can easily make the mistake of thinking that they *know*. Socrates (469?-399 B.C.E.) said, "I know nothing except the fact of my ignorance."[16]

Tao is not within the realm of things known, but pertains to what the ancients termed "no-mind" or "Buddha-Mind,"[17] not a platform for self-promotion, spiritual one-upmanship, hierarchical attitudes, or pedantry. Tao has been referred to as the watercourse way—water does not strive; it flows to lower places.[18] Sages teach that inner peace comes with an attitude of inclusiveness, love, and humble witness to the mystery of "the inexpressible."

MISSING VALUES

Abraham Maslow (1908-1970), who coined such expressions as "self-actualization" and "peak experience," is considered the founder of humanistic psychology in the West. He believed that the ultimate disease of our times is a lack of values. "The cure for this disease is obvious," he said. "We need a validated, usable system of human values, values that we can believe in and devote ourselves to because they are true rather than because we are exhorted to 'believe and have faith.'"[19] "Valuing the whole" satisfies this criterion. Maslow observed,

> The teaching of spiritual values or ethical and moral values definitely does (in principle) have a place in education, perhaps ultimately a very basic and essential place, and . . . this in no way needs to controvert the American separation between church and state for the very simple reason that spiritual, ethical, and moral values need have nothing to do with any church. Or perhaps, better said, they are the common core of all churches, all religions, including the non-theistic ones.[20]

INEXPERIENCE WITH WHOLENESS

Many people sense a void in their lives, an absence of purpose or meaning. Both education and counseling can address this situation. As people learn about wholeness and experience it directly, personal transformation occurs. A psychological/spiritual window opens and purpose appears or is rekindled. As one group of students at an alternative high school learned about the holistic options that already exist for humanity's success, in one hour their collective attitude transformed from lethargy, apathy, and cynicism to excitement, relief, and hope for the future. Although lack of hope is a common denominator for many people today, this outlook can change very quickly. *The energies associated with the direct experience of wholeness are transformative.*

The Role of Mythology

A myth is commonly defined as an invented story or idea, a person or thing that is imaginary or fictitious. Its primary definition, however, is "a traditional or legendary story, usually concerning some being or hero or event, with or without a determinable basis of fact or a natural explanation, especially one that is concerned with deities or demigods and explains some practice, rite, or phenomenon of nature."[21]

The scholar and mythologist Joseph Campbell (1904-1987) reminded us that every culture throughout human history has had a distinctive mythology—stories communicated to successive generations that define and sustain the society's basic values and ways of life. A culture's mythology is vitally important because myths are "clues to the spiritual potentialities of the human life."[22] Religion presents an obvious parallel. Campbell said, "Each religion is a kind of software; it has its own set of signals. . . ."[23] He pointed to the *Star Wars* movies as a good example of popular mythology: the struggle of good versus evil, the phenomena of epic love and friendship, the search for meaning in life, the wisdom of the guru.

Erosion of the nuclear family, skepticism about traditional religion, and the decimation of native cultures (among other factors) have created a situation in which many people have no guiding mythology in their lives, leaving them psychologically and spiritually unsatisfied.

Myths can be evaluated in light of the cultural benefits they provide. Campbell said that their basic benefit is "opening the world to the dimension of mystery," enabling people "to realize the mystery that underlies all forms." Without that function, there is no mythology. Mystery opens us to wonder and possibility, beyond what is already known. Campbell also revealed the cosmological aspect of myths: "seeing that mystery as manifest through all things, so the universe becomes, as it were, a holy picture—you are always addressed to the transcendent mysteries through that."[24]

Another beneficial function of mythology, according to Campbell, is to validate and maintain a society by conveying its ethical laws, values, and codes of behavior. A further service of mythology is to provide life models that show "how to live a human lifetime under any circumstances." Campbell observed that "the moral order has to catch up with the moral necessities of actual life in time, here and now." Although certain values are universal and eternal, he emphasized that life models "have to be appropriate to the possibilities of the time in which you are living. And our time has changed and continues to change so fast that what was proper fifty years ago is not proper today."[25]

Society is in need of an inclusive model—one that can be held sacred by religionists *and* valued by secularists—a guiding metaphor, an authentic mythology that can provide the benefits outlined by Campbell. While some believe that conditions are changing too rapidly for a "new" mythology to appear, perhaps there is a "fixed star," a "known horizon,"[26] that could help people anchor their lives in today's complex and often overwhelming world.

Modern communication and transportation, as well as economic and environmental concerns, already join all humans in a "global village."[27] Therefore, a mythology appropriate for our times would have to appeal worldwide. Such a mythology would encompass and transcend the myriad ethnicities, religions, nationalisms, and self-interests, at the same time recognizing and honoring individual and cultural differences. What mythology could fulfill all of these requirements while providing a model of "how to live a human lifetime"?

The story of wholeness. Its mysteries, values, and teachings provide not only a basis for unity but an arena for realizing the potentialities of human life. This *living* mythology could become the story communicated to successive generations.

Upon connecting with wholeness, the "otherness" of people and the rest of nature vanishes. As changes in consciousness occur, "the other" comes to be seen as an aspect of one's own self. Campbell said that society arrives at a "totally different civilization, a totally different way of living" according to its myth depending on whether nature ("the other") is regarded as fallen or as divine—"the Spirit being the revelation of the Divinity that is inherent in nature."[28]

Campbell also noted that a myth for our times would have to "incorporate the machine just as the old myths incorporated the tools that people used."[29] In this context, Buckminster Fuller's holistic approach to technology and design takes on added significance.

Buckminster Fuller and Tao

Fuller, whose inventions are patterned upon the design principles of nature, did refer to Taoist and other Eastern philosophies.[30] Baldwin recounts, "When a student jokingly asked if the ultimate more-with-less was to do everything-with-nothing, Bucky said yes: Design is at its best the closer it approaches the purely metaphysical."[31]

In a prose poem Fuller wrote, "the real beginning of education / must be the experimental realization / of absolute mystery."[32] He once said, "The a priori chemical, electromagnetic, atomistic, genetic, and synergetic designing . . . apparently was instituted by a wisdom—a formulative capability inherent in Universe—higher than that possessed by any known living humans."[33] When asked if *Universe* and *God* meant the same thing, he replied, "God seems like a rather small concept to contain the exquisitely interaccommodative coherencies of Universe."[34] A master holistic educator, Fuller always returned to the wonder and mystery of the whole:

> I am o'erwhelmed by the only experientially discovered evidence of an a priori eternal, omnicomprehensive, infinitely and exquisitely concerned, intellectual integrity that we *may* call God, though knowing that in whatever way we humans refer to this integrity, it will always be an inadequate expression of its cosmic omniscience and omnipotence.[35]

A key word in this quotation is "experientially." Interpretations of "the inexpressible" are unnecessary, since it is experienced directly through, for example, stillness, receptivity, love, and service. Fuller's reference to an "inadequate expression" brings to mind the first lines of the *Tao Te Ching,* by Lao-tzu:

> The tao that can be told is not the eternal Tao.
> The name that can be named is not the eternal name.[36]

Since much of education does occur through words, Fuller sometimes referred to the "Greater Intellectual Integrity."[37] Careful not to anthropomorphize, he stated, "Acknowledging the mathematically elegant intellectual integrity of eternally regenerative Universe is one way of identifying God."[38] The mathematical elegance of this integrity is demonstrated throughout Fuller's work. This is not to say that he believed the universe is determined and regulated by some eternal, mathematical supermind; he simply affirmed that behind the apparent chaos and randomness in life, coherent organizing principles and order are evident.[39]

Tao in Business and Government

One of the greatest untold news stories of our time is that humanity possesses a multitude of holistic options in every field of endeavor and for every area of the environment that has been compromised. The existence of these options, however, does not mean they have been valued and implemented on a broad scale. The present mindset of business, government, and the media is far too reductionist.

Corporate policymakers operate within time frames imposed by quarterly and annual earning reports; government officials must demonstrate success before the next election; immediate results are often required in order to hold one's job, receive better offers, or be reelected. Due to these and other factors, people wielding the most power in society are blind to the whole[40] and hence to options that could lead us out of our present predicament.

In practical terms, how could the holistic approach be translated into action, if the need were seen? Due to the nature of holism and synergy, it would be extremely inefficient to establish holistic policies in one area of life without simultaneously addressing all other areas, since all are interconnected. For example, pertaining to the environmental sector: protecting biodiversity, phasing out dependence on unsafe agricultural and other chemicals, reducing air and water pollution, banning the manufacture of chemical and nuclear weapons, phasing out fossil fuels and nuclear energy, replanting forests, and rebuilding topsoil must be regarded as a *single worldwide endeavor.* Similarly, the sectors themselves—environmental, economic, social, etc.—also interconnect and need to be addressed as one. Holistic education is the key to such perceptions and actions. Within an organization, holistic values need to permeate all areas including manufacturing, marketing, research and development, public relations, human resources, job training and professional development, accounting, investments, legal affairs, and environmental policies.

In cultures where personal growth and free expression are subordinated to nationalism and commercialism, holistic education is especially needed. What could motivate corporate directors and their political allies—whose policies dictate the direction of events that can determine whether ecosystems live or die—to learn about and apply the principles of holism?

Those in command of supranational corporations are driven to maximize profits and to consolidate their power and control (among other motivations). Can they be persuaded that greater profits are possible by practicing environmental conservation and restoration rather than extraction and exploitation? For example, rain forest plants can be used for medicines, foods, dyes, fibers, oils, rubber, cosmetics, crafts, solvents, pesticides, and a host of other nontimber products—not to mention the intrinsic value of rain forests and the fact that they are home for the greatest portion of the world's biodiversity. Over the long term, cultivating in a nondepleting way creates far more monetary value than cattle ranching, strip mining, or one-time timber sales.[41] (It is argued that commercial enterprises should not be vilified since they merely respond to consumer demands for such things as tropical hardwood products and cheaper meat. Many of these demands, however, are created and sustained by corporations in the first place. While some deforestation is caused by subsistence farmers, their plight often stems from prevailing economic policies.) The sociological and political issues underlying deforestation and other environmental problems are so widespread and complex that only the holistic approach is capable of responding to the crisis of perception and values illustrated in Capra's chart in appendix E.

Living in tune with Tao implies action proportionate to the requirements of the moment. The invented systems that have brought humanity to its present predicament must be rethought. A shift in the habits and underlying psychology of a civilization is indicated. This complex but not impossible task is already underway, in large part through the efforts of concerned individuals and holistically oriented Civic Society Organizations (CSOs)[42] worldwide, as well as through some governments and corporations.

Business and government can and do change when necessary, or when the citizenry demands it.[43] History is rife with paradigm shifts. As the ongoing holistic paradigm shift gains momentum, "we the people," individually and collectively, will have increasing opportunities to act upon and base our consumer decisions upon holistic options.

Education in the "subject" of wholeness will help corporate policymakers and government officials recognize the interconnectedness of all life—including the fact that a rain forest is worth more alive than dead. This key point illustrates the importance of integrating wholeness into every domain of education and public consciousness. The historian of cultures Thomas Berry states,

> The natural world itself is the primary economic reality, the primary educator, the primary governance, the primary healer, the primary presence of the sacred, the primary moral value. . . .
>
> The ecology issue is not for some one course in education. It is the course, the curriculum, the structure of the whole business. It is the background for medicine, it is the preparation for law. It is not a course; it is *the* course.[44]

Many individuals, organizations, and societies today can be considered hypermaterialistic. Long ago, Chuang-tzu described what happens when only external realities are valued:

> When he tries to extend his power
> Over objects,
> Those objects gain control
> Of him.
> He who is controlled by objects
> Loses possession of his inner self:
> If he no longer values himself,
> How can he value others?
> If he no longer values others,
> He is abandoned.
> He has nothing left![45]

A paradigm of reality based on an economic system of constant growth is not the best matrix for looking at and living life. The *Tao Te Ching* says,

> Better stop short than fill to the brim.
> Oversharpen the blade, and the edge will soon blunt.[46]

With their global networks, large supranational companies could choose to be among the leaders in reversing environmental devastation; instead, lacking the holistic values that would link economic policies with ecology and ethics,[47] many of these institutions remain the biggest contributors to the tragedy. India's great poet Rabindranath Tagore (1861-1941) wrote,

The clumsiness of power spoils the key,
and uses the pickaxe.[48]

A holistic governance of a free society would be truly represen-
tative, benign, synergistic, and not based on personalities—a system
wherein communities and citizens had greater control over their own
lives. Some form of transnational, measured rule is needed, if only to
ensure that we do not ruin the remaining life-support systems of
Earth, but such a governance must be committed to the well-being
of all. (When more people are holistically educated, it will be easier
to agree on what constitutes "well-being.")

Frogs

An aspect of Tao, as mentioned, pertains to action proportionate
to the requirements of the moment. But what if we are unable to
perceive the requirements of the moment? Many are familiar with
the parable involving frogs placed in a pan of cold water. When the
water was gradually brought to a boil, the frogs didn't become
alarmed, didn't jump out, and eventually boiled to death.[49]

Humanity still hasn't realized that the pan (Earth) has been
gradually heating up, so we (the frogs) haven't jumped out of this
danger into a more viable paradigm. Awakening to wholeness can
remedy our collective lack of perception. Holistic education is a
tool—a microscope/telescope combination perfectly suited for
"home laboratory" use—for helping individuals gain insight into
environmental, social, economic, and political conditions, as well as
personal issues.

How fast are attitudes changing? Are holistically sound decisions
being implemented through international agreements? How about
governmental policies at national, regional, and local levels? Are
holistically oriented CSOs being given the support they need and are

their methods and successes being adequately communicated? For example, although some progress has been made in creating recycling and other conservation programs, advancing alternative healthcare, building energy-efficient structures, and establishing cooperatives, only a tiny fraction of the available holistic options are being utilized to any appreciable extent.

As numerous "canaries in the coal mine" continue to expire before our eyes (to mix metaphors), the "boiled frog" phenomenon has kept us from acting with the necessary urgency. Many personal problems (regarding addiction, abuse, attitude, etc.) are also related to this situation. Only through the inception of holistic education throughout the world can we shift the immense psychological inertia of our present reductionist mindset.

The Philosopher Is In—*You*

When people discover the existence of the whole, it is then their prerogative to become self-educated in the "subject" and to discover practical ways of applying holistic principles to daily life. Collective and personal circumstances suggest that each of us become a "holistic philosopher" with respect to our life choices and in our relationships with others. The future of humanity depends upon people everywhere learning to relate holistically. Hence, the philosopher is in—*you*.

Some companies employ "greenwashing," public relations campaigns designed to create perceptions of environmental friendliness. Similarly, some teachers, doctors, and others assert that they are holistic when their actions (and/or products) reveal otherwise. Learning about and experiencing wholeness helps one to discern qualified holistic professionals in the fields of healthcare, education, counseling, the environment, economics, business, and government.

Holistic principles can be discovered in numerous ways, such as: observation of and interaction with nature; meditation; participation in yoga, tai chi chuan, and similar activities; association with holistically oriented people; interaction with cultures that have applied holistic principles for millennia; study of the teachings of sages and the example of their lives; and consideration of our own intuition.

Spending a few years on a holistic self-education project (allowing periods of time to integrate the information, experiences, and insights) may seem like a huge undertaking, but the *nearness* and relevance of the "subject" of wholeness ensures that many rewards (tangible and intangible) will appear from the outset. Although the books listed in appendix B will be helpful, a holistic orientation comes experientially, intuitively, and spontaneously.

Out of the Formless Comes Form

The *Tao Te Ching* tells us,

> Returning is the motion of the Tao.
> Yielding is the way of the Tao.
> The ten thousand things are born of being.
> Being is born of not being.[50]

We usually spend our time interacting with various forms, the objects and events in our lives. When one also connects with the formless—streaming with Tao, so to speak—a certain resonance with life, a vitality and balance appear. People thus connected cannot help demonstrating that they value, indeed love, the whole. As many have noted, only by emptying oneself of fixation on forms (the parts) can one be filled. Through meditation (whether sitting cross-legged or not, eyes closed or open), nonbeneficial patterns of thinking drop away, bringing profound calmness, joy, and respite from the restless mind. The Third Zen Patriarch, Sengtsan (c. 551 C.E.; known in Japan as Sosan), said,

> Emptiness here, Emptiness there,
> but the infinite universe stands
> always before your eyes.
> Infinitely large and infinitely small:
> no difference, for definitions have vanished
> and no boundaries are seen.[51]

A time-honored way to meditate is simply to sit and remain still, "watching" one's own breath. Soon, the watcher recedes and "the inexpressible" remains. The *Tao Te Ching* explains,

> Since before time and space were,
> the Tao is.
> It is beyond *is* and *is not*.
> How do I know this is true?
> I look inside myself and see.[52]

Not long after bringing meditation into daily living, one begins to observe one's everyday thoughts, emotions, attitudes, and behaviors with heightened clarity and insight. What once were big problems become less and less so.

Wholeness is necessarily "generic," and available to all. It can be experienced through meditation, sitting quietly, and connecting with nature just by walking out-of-doors or gardening, for example. If one chooses to meditate, there is no organization one must join or doctrine to accept. Anyone can "learn how" in a few minutes. However, in the spiritual marketplace caution is called for when groups offer "the one true path" to greater accomplishment and inner peace. If substantial funds are required in order to learn how to sit and watch inwardly, or ever-higher "levels" of saintliness are available for ever-higher fees, take heed. Although people manifest oneness in widely varying degrees, when examined in the purest light oneness has no levels. Since ancient times, sages have taught that this is an ordinary state of being. As with sunshine and rain, it costs nothing to experience.

While generally ignoring the formless, most systems of education emphasize only the outer realm of form. Education and philosophy, when infused with holistic consciousness, move beyond "talk about preexisting talk." Normally a "doing," education becomes a function of *being*. Whether communing with students, creating lesson plans, or interacting with parents and faculty, teachers will find that perfect actions, ideas, expressions, and solutions appear when they regard the world holistically and honor Spirit within all. This is Tao in action and applies in every domain of life. If people are taught only about forms, how can they ever realize wholeness? The *Tao Te Ching* illustrates,

> We join spokes together in a wheel,
> but it is the center hole
> that makes the wagon move.
>
> We shape clay into a pot,
> but it is the emptiness inside
> that holds whatever we want.
>
> We hammer wood for a house,
> but it is the inner space
> that makes it livable.
>
> We work with being,
> but non-being is what we use.[53]

The Elusive Unified Theory

In the ongoing quest to advance our knowledge of the universe, particle physicists have sought to identify the smallest, most fundamental particles that make up matter and to understand their interactions. During recent decades, ever-more-sophisticated experiments have led to the discovery of smaller and smaller particles, with quarks and leptons currently reigning as the smallest of the small. The so-called Standard Model describes this subatomic world for the most part, and numerous experiments continue to validate this approach.[54] But the Standard Model does not account for every phenomenon, which forces scientists to consider whether there might be yet smaller particles.

In particular, the Standard Model accounts for the interactions associated with only three of the four known physical forces: electromagnetism and the strong and weak nuclear forces, but not gravity.[55] The search for a single model that accounts for all physical interactions, a Unified Theory (sometimes called the Theory of Everything), is a top priority in modern science.

Not surprisingly, there is considerable disagreement about what constitutes a Theory of Everything. A truly *unified* theory would be holistic—encompassing areas within the physical and biological sciences as well as areas outside them like philosophy, sociology, religion, history, education, and metaphysics. Such a holistic theory might appear to be "mathematically elegant" (Buckminster Fuller's words pertaining to the "intellectual integrity of eternally regenerative Universe"), would demonstrate synergy, and would be encompassed by the intuitive, spiritual realm that is nonquantifiable and undefinable. It is fitting that an intuitive approach is required for investigating this all-inclusiveness.

In the *Tao Te Ching* it is said,

> The Tao begot one.
> One begot two.
> Two begot three.
> And three begot the ten thousand things.[56]

No matter how finely instruments may eventually measure phenomena and to what degree scientists may refine particles into more elementary ones (atoms, protons, neutrons, electrons, quarks, superstrings[57]—smaller, smaller, smaller), the basic component cannot be pinned down. This is true by definition because the whole, the ultimate unity—Tao—that is everything (and every no-thing), also includes the formless realm. Indeed, the whole is where form and formless transcend all differentiation. Of course, these are merely labels, after-the-fact mental constructs. "The inexpressible" remains inexpressible.

It is easy to become distracted by a reductionist impulse to define, quantify, and understand the infinite. In philosophical, psychological, and theological sectors, the "let's find the ever more elementary particle and all-encompassing theory" approach is reflected in numerous pronouncements about the "true nature" of life, consciousness, or Creation. Those philosophers, theologians, scientists, and others who attempt to elucidate the mystery of the whole at best provide information about it *in vitro.* Alternatively, the ancient sages suggested that we tune in to the whole, where form and formless are one, open to *that* unity and instantly *be that*—experiencing oneness directly, letting the inner mystic, philosopher, and poet unfold the way.

It can be argued that "experiencing oneness directly" is self-delusion; thought forms can be quite subtle, misleading some into believing they are experiencing wholeness when they may be engaging in an intellectual exercise or hallucinating to some degree. The "concept" of wholeness itself is a qualifier; the discourse or even thinking about it sets up duality—the subject-object axis. In this respect, terminology and even *ideas* like meditation, spirit, and God can become barriers. While these points are valid, so is the reality of stillness and wholeness that transcends the thinking mind. The *Tao Te Ching* says,

> The Tao is nowhere to be found.
> Yet it nourishes and completes all things.[58]

Objective reality (so called) has its place, but it is not the whole any more than visible light is the entire electromagnetic spectrum. When the fifteenth-century Zen master Ikkyū expressed the following sentiment, he may have been referring to the unending human propensity to try to explain the unexplainable Divine Mystery:

> hear the cruel no-answer until blood drips down
> beat your head against the wall of it.[59]

The ancient *rishis* simply indicated that when we open to the eternal mystery within and without, the way appears.

The reductionist approach to life and learning has limitations. While seeking the ultimate theory, or Theory of Everything, scientists have generally focused on individual components such as waves, particles, fields, and strings. Discoveries await those who center on, and with, the unity, the whole.

Love is the key to wholeness. It expresses the unity in a single experience that is subatomic, astronomic, electromagnetic, gravitational, chemical, biological, psychological, interpersonal, multidimensional, mystical.

Tao could also be used to designate the "ultimate unified theory" of the sciences, social sciences, humanities, spirituality, religion, all living things, galaxies, and space: all that is, or isn't. Kabir, a fifteenth-century Indian mystic and poet, put it this way:

> Thinkers, listen, tell me what you know of that is not
>   inside the soul?
> Take a pitcher full of water and set it down on the
>   water—
> now it has water inside and water outside.
> We mustn't give it a name,
> lest silly people start talking again about the body and
>   the soul.
>
> If you want the truth, I'll tell you the truth:
> Listen to the secret sound, the real sound, which is
>   inside you.[60]

Neuron Pathways

Scientists are finding that neurons in the brain can grow or shrink. New neuron pathways (threadlike connections between neurons) can be established and old pathways strengthened. In other words, our brain circuitry seems to be in a continual process of "rewiring."[61] Who is responsible for initiating and directing this rewiring? Ideally, the individual. If one is not alert, however, the rewiring can be directed without our knowledge by people, events, or allurements outside ourselves (i.e., mental programming).

As people come into wholeness, intuition is heightened and they become more discerning. With wholeness as the foundation, the actual context of things and events is perceived more accurately. The faculty of internal and external pattern recognition also becomes enhanced, increasing insight into which outcomes are likely to result from which actions. For example, if our collective sense of pattern recognition were better developed, we would already be using such energy technologies as solar panels, wind turbines, and hydrogen fuel cells in every possible application.

When individuals decide to honor the formless (instead of being incessantly occupied with various forms) and act in accord with the holistic reality, then neurons become attuned to wholeness. Such attunement can happen quickly or over time, perhaps during a program of holistic self-education. Purposefully nurtured, holistically "rewired" neuron pathways and receptor sites beget more of the same.

Our Common Ground

Fragmentation and discord are epidemic in today's society. Though there are innumerable subjects about which individuals, families, ethnic groups, organizations, governments, and religions vehemently disagree, some issues can be agreed upon. Along with personal differences and seemingly intractable global problems come a few universal truths with respect to human behavior.

People of all cultures generally value family, friends, good manners, and quality workmanship. All humans desire clean water and air. Everyone can appreciate a refreshing breeze on a hot day. Sages throughout history have taught that humans possess an innate capacity to experience another sort of ever-present "breeze"— wholeness.

In everyday life, trying to agree on our common ground can be a challenge. For example, even environmentalists disagree over policy. They may believe that remedial action is necessary, but there is considerable debate about how to proceed and with what degree of urgency. How can we best live in harmony with the environment? Should we continue with the transnational-corporate, top-down, insider-driven, mega-project approach (to energy, agriculture, etc.), or is a bioregional and point-of-use approach preferable? The environment is only one of many subjects in which there is raging disagreement among scientists, academicians, politicians, and many others. Ironically, a lack of awareness about what constitutes our common ground is one of the things we have in common.

There is no contradiction between valuing oneness and respecting cultural and individual differences. Throughout the world, people share common experiences in connection with the environment, communication, transportation, business, economics, art, literature, music, entertainment, sports, architecture, inventions, food, healthcare, disease, and human rights. Now, the all-important philosophical world view—our de facto oneness and interconnections—needs to be explicitly identified and nurtured as our fundamental common ground, the whole. As more individuals come to value and live this reality, society will become transformed.

A Personal Decision

Returning to the questions posed in the first chapter: As we move into the twenty-first century, what kind of world do we really want? What options are available? How should we be educating ourselves and our children? What unifying ethic could benefit all life on the planet? Is there some specific knowledge that can help us determine for ourselves viable answers to these questions? Becoming attuned to wholeness will enhance our ability to discern and to be optimally effective in dealing with our most vexing personal and collective problems.

History teaches that the "right" way has never been the exclusive domain of any person, group, tribe, race, or religion. Over the centuries, authentic wisdom, inspired narratives, and profound discoveries have emerged from every culture. Judgments based on place of birth or skin color evaporate when wholeness and the invisible realm are valued. The number of concerned, holistically oriented people is growing, and nurturing this trend should be one of our highest priorities.

Living in the now opens the way. For example, a slight attention shift may bring awareness of a bird calling, a clock ticking, noise from passing cars, a fragrance, the feel of the sun or breeze. Being receptive, one can become motionless, aware of the breath—being *here,* softly gazing into space or closing the eyes, then forgetting the breath and floating with "the inexpressible."

The ancient Buddhas called it *tathatā* ("suchness"), which is "immutable, immovable, and beyond all concepts and distinctions."[62] The hope for humanity rests on wholeness. Nature—exquisitely informed, everywhere present—is the instructive manifestation. Art, Science, Poetry, and Beauty are here. The infinitely complex, infinitely simple, and infinitely sublime are here. Everything cherished and loved is here. Holistic awareness illuminates specific strategies and actions necessary for healing the individual, society, and the ecosystem. Buckminster Fuller observed,

> Humanity is now maintaining an unstable collection of local holding patterns, awaiting a physical or metaphysical integrity to give structure to the future and to show the way out of the darkness. The twentieth century's leap into a realm with a million times greater range of reality, produced by the sudden visibility and employability of the total electromagnetic spectrum, has brought humans to the edge of self-extinction for lack of adequate guiding forces. Big business and big religion's inclination for moneymaking and power has served only to foster the continuance of a millennium of isolation, inhumanity, misinformation, and ignorance.

> We now have available to each of us the comprehensive information that can lead us out of the Dark Ages, which continue to hold

us down with physical and moral barriers to the free flow of the information and materials that would spontaneously liberate us. The old
structures were prejudicial human physical-power structures. The
adamantine new structure is metaphysical, pristine, eternal, a generalized system of pure principle.[63]

Wholeness

World society has not yet evolved an appropriate understanding of
how to coexist with the planet and with itself. We perpetuate an economic system predicated on dismantling the very environment upon
which we all depend. This system encourages and amplifies the
worst character traits of human beings and, in our ignorance, we
have reached the point where Earth's life-support capabilities are
endangered. At the top of the food chain, humans have become the
ultimate predator—some purposefully, others unconsciously by
default, merely trying to survive.

Today as the world's human population exceeds six billion,
people at every level of society continue to behave according to the
ancient biological/psychological encodement "to be predatory, to
extract and devour," a way of life that may have been necessary for
survival in some cultures in times past. But now living conditions
are different. Certain behaviors, the burning of fossil fuels being one
example among many, are simply no longer appropriate on a planet
with six billion people. As a society we cannot continue to allow
essential ecosystems to be destroyed.

Yet, options exist. Fossil fuels and nuclear energy can be replaced
by more benign sources. Trees and other biomass could be planted
on a massive scale to absorb carbon dioxide. Depleted soils can be
remineralized with rock dust as an alternative to chemical fertilizers
and pesticides.[64] Alternative sources of fiber for pulp can be used
to manufacture paper and paperboard products; "woodless lumber"
can be used for building. The world's militaries could become the

world's environmental restoration corps—*and* education can become concerned with the whole, not just the parts. The environment can be *allowed* to recover, where still possible. We can perceive ourselves as, and act as, a single world society—aboard an integral, biological Spaceship Earth. Much of what needs to be done, what demonstrably can be done, and what should not be done is already known (see appendix B).

The most comprehensive task facing us is gaining a holistic orientation, and then helping to refocus the perceptions and values of an entire society. How can this occur? Naturally, the practical, everyday expressions of holistic philosophy will be unique to each individual. Discovering what these are *is* the awakening to wholeness. Many people would like a recipe to be provided by some leader, teacher, organization, or book, but the integration can only be personal. When the holistic orientation is present, what to do (and what not to do) becomes clear.

In order to learn about a particular perspective, people must first be exposed to it. Although the experience of wholeness is personal, it is also collective. The logistics are already in place to help swiftly raise humanity's consciousness of the whole, if we so desire. There have been countless instances in the past when people have come together for the common good.

The environmental crisis and most personal and societal dysfunction are the result of falling away from wholeness. Connecting to wholeness means honoring the formless, nonquantifiable realm—in an immediate way that is not overlaid by any particular religion or system of belief. The realm of form accounts for only a tiny slice of reality. The sciences, social sciences, and our business, economic, and education systems need to evolve beyond their exclusive attachment to the parts and embrace "the inexpressible" whole as everyday objective reality—present, recognizable, and operational.

Consciousness can enable one to transcend outmoded biological and psychological "imperatives." Consciousness of what? The answer is for each individual to determine, and awakening to wholeness can help one make that determination. *The energies associated with the direct experience of wholeness are universally transformative.*

The first sentence of the *Tao Te Ching* states, "The tao that can be told is not the eternal Tao." It has been said that the entire truth of the *Tao* resides in this single expression and everything that follows is mere commentary. Unlike all that can be learned through books or lectures, wholeness cannot be explained, and one should be wary of anyone purporting to do so. The essence of Buddha's final teaching: be a light unto thyself.

Although the eternal Tao cannot be told, the connections are ours to make.

OM
That is the Whole.
This is the Whole.
From wholeness emerges wholeness.
Wholeness coming from wholeness,
   wholeness still remains.

ISA UPANISHAD

Appendix A

Reference Outlines for Courses

The concepts presented in this book are integrated into the following outlines. Since experiencing wholeness occurs in a broader context than learning about it in a formulaic or linear fashion, these outlines are intended only as guides in designing courses on holism and the work of R. Buckminster Fuller.[1]

As mentioned in the text, wholeness is not a subject in the usual sense and cannot be defined, explained, or learned; yet there are things *about* it that can be learned. This central paradox will continue to surface. Wholeness is a state of being, an experience, a perspective, and cannot be reduced to reference outlines or courses.

I.

TOPIC **Wholeness**

DESCRIPTION

For centuries, the three Rs (reading, writing, and arithmetic) have been considered the pillars of education. But there is a (metaphorical) fourth "R" that pertains to wholeness—the interconnectedness of creation, the oneness of being. Just as reading and writing require knowledge of words and sentence structure, and arithmetic involves multiplication and division, this fourth "R," wholeness (which may really be the first "R"), has its own fundamentals. While the three Rs are learnable skills, wholeness refers to the totality. The "fourth R" metaphor merely signifies that wholeness, in addition to meaning "everything," is one of the basics of education. (If an actual R word is desired, use *relatedness*.)

An interdisciplinary course on the "subject" of wholeness examines its components, significance, and practical applications, including historical background and philosophical context. Many teachers already use an interdisciplinary approach; however, the main purpose of this course is to advance awareness of wholeness *itself* as a "subject." This is a key point.

"Holistic" refers to the natural, organic, functional relationship between the whole and the parts. Global changes, contemporary education philosophy, the work of Buckminster Fuller, and the philosophy of Tao are among the areas investigated.

OBJECTIVES

To gain a comprehensive understanding of the theory and practical applications of holism. To explore its ancient philosophical and spiritual foundations. To acquire an appreciation of new physics and developments in the other sciences that provide contemporary theoretical underpinnings for the holistic paradigm. To be able to analyze and critique holism from a variety of perspectives. To learn effective ways of communicating with others about the "subject" of wholeness. To return the spark to education (where needed) and to explore ways of sharing it.

READING[2] In addition to *Wholeness: On Education, Buckminster Fuller, and Tao*, select a number of books from the following (and from the other books listed in appendix B):

> *Betrayal of Science and Reason: How Anti-Environmental Rhetoric Threatens Our Future*, by Paul R. Ehrlich and Anne H. Ehrlich
> *The Book of Leadership and Strategy: Lessons of the Chinese Masters*, translated by Thomas Cleary
> *Bucky Works: Buckminster Fuller's Ideas for Today*, by J. Baldwin
> *The Chalice and the Blade: Our History, Our Future*, by Riane Eisler
> *Critical Path*, by Buckminster Fuller (with Kiyoshi Kuromiya, adjuvant)
> *Ecological Literacy: Education and the Transition to a Postmodern World*, by David W. Orr
> *Education and the Significance of Life*, by J. Krishnamurti
> *The Enlightened Heart: An Anthology of Sacred Poetry*, edited by Stephen Mitchell
> *Gaia: The Human Journey from Chaos to Cosmos*, by Elisabet Sahtouris
> *The Great Work: Our Way into the Future*, by Thomas Berry
> *The Heat Is On: The High Stakes Battle over Earth's Threatened Climate*, by Ross Gelbspan
> *The New Biology: Discovering the Wisdom in Nature*, by Robert Augros and George Stanciu
> *Tao Te Ching*, by Lao-tzu[3]
> *The Turning Point: Science, Society, and the Rising Culture*, by Fritjof Capra
> *The Way of Chuang Tzu*, by Thomas Merton
> *The Web of Life: A New Scientific Understanding of Living Systems*, by Fritjof Capra
> *Tomorrow's Children: A Blueprint for Partnership Education in the 21st Century*, by Riane Eisler

TOPIC OUTLINE (based on *Wholeness: On Education, Buckminster Fuller, and Tao*)

Introduction: a context for education about wholeness
> Definitions: wholeness ("entirety," "totality")—a quality of being, an experience (book knowledge being only part of the whole)

Significance of the topic

The environmental mandate

>Union of Concerned Scientists' "World Scientists' Warning to Humanity"

>U.N. Intergovernmental Panel on Climate Change announcements

>Buckminster Fuller's warnings

>Jacques Cousteau's last warning

>Recent books concerning climate change and the environment (see appendix B)

>Test-tube Earth; momentum (regarding environmental degradation and psychological inertia); the "boiled frog" phenomenon[4]

>Where the environment connects to other sectors

Fragmentation, cognitive discord, disconnection, denial, fundamentalism, valuelessness; a "crisis of perception and values"[5]

Options

>Which blueprint to use in creating a better world?

>Optimal effectiveness (especially with the faculty of discernment)

>"Comprehensivity" (Buckminster Fuller's use of the term; also his teaching, "To be optimally effective, undertake at outset the most comprehensive task in the most comprehensive and incisively detailed manner")[6]

>Holism: not simply another "ism," but a tool for discerning among the numerous "isms"

>The experience of wholeness

Integrity: "the state of being whole, entire, or undiminished"[7]

Features of holism:

A. Synergy: one introduction to holism

>Definitions, basic components, significance, examples and practical applications

B. Whole-to-parts orientation

>Learning to think and act from the whole to the particulars and why this is important

>*Holistic orientation,* a tool for enhancing the ability to discern

>Authors/teachers in the field of holism; related issues

>The ancient philosophy of Tao and its relevance today

>Critique of holism; no need to defend possessing a toolbox

C. The invisible realm

>Invisible processes affect much of life

>Many environmental problems are invisible

>"Objective proof required" syndrome

>Intuition and emotional connection

>Compassion and love

D. The paradigm shift

    Paradigm shifts throughout history

    Reductionism, historical and contemporary

    Holism, historical and contemporary

        Holism: a metaphilosophy, a philosophy of philosophy

        Current intellectual climate regarding holism

        Holistic approach in education, economics, design, health, and other fields

E. Practical applications of holism

    Two primary aspects

        Personally learning about and connecting with the whole

        Investigating holistic strategies and artifacts that have practical, timely application in the world

    Holistic orientation, in itself a practical step

    Learning about and taking advantage of synergy

    Learning about and attempting to live principles of Tao

        Introduction to Tao ("the inexpressible"): what is it? why Tao? the perennial philosophy,[8] wonderment, compassion, Tao in education

    Mythology and the work of Joseph Campbell

    A mythology for our times

    Options for humanity (e.g., artifacts and strategies of Buckminster Fuller)

    Practical applications of holistic principles are possible in every field (e.g., alternative sources of raw material used to manufacture paper, paperboard, and wood products; "woodless lumber" for building)

    Holistic education

        Transmission of wisdom from generation to generation

        What constitutes "wisdom" today?

        Applications of holistic principles in the classroom

        How to create a holistic curriculum for each grade level

        Experiential activities

        Teacher education

        Education of administrators, staff, aides, parents, and volunteers

F. Valuing the whole (e.g., the universe, Earth, all forms of life)

    A unifying ethic

    Spirituality

    An apolitical, secular and/or interdenominational touchstone for evaluating education, environmental and governmental policies, etc.

    Holistic values and the unification of ecology, economics, and ethics[9]

    The self-fulfilling prophecy related to personal vision and growth

Beyond ideology
    What are the essential questions of our time?
    What kind of world do we want?
    What options are available?
    What is the role of education?
    What isn't being discussed that should be?
    What are the implications of the holistic paradigm?
    Holistic resources
G. The role of intuition
    Moving beyond the words

II.

TOPIC R. Buckminster Fuller

DESCRIPTION

Buckminster Fuller (1895-1983) was an engineer, designer, architect, geometrician, cartographer, poet, philosopher, and educator. He coined the term "Spaceship Earth" and is perhaps best known for the geodesic dome. Described as "the Leonardo da Vinci of our times" and "the planet's friendly genius,"[10] Fuller espoused a holistic philosophy that provides both objective and intuitively perceived links among the sciences, technology, and the social sciences. To Fuller, "There is always only one topic: the universe—whole systems."[11] His comprehensive philosophy addresses some of the most vexing issues regarding education (including curriculum, relevance, boredom, and burnout), the environment, energy, shelter, economics, and government. This course presents a detailed study of Buckminster Fuller's contributions and their relevance.

OBJECTIVES

To systematically study the applied philosophy of one of our most inventive and important thinkers. To explore the significance of "education for comprehensivity."[12] To examine ideas that can be of practical value in one's personal life and in the fields of design, education, ecology, economics, government, ethics, whole systems, etc.

READING[13]

BuckyWorks: Buckminster Fuller's Ideas for Today, by J. Baldwin
Critical Path, by Buckminster Fuller (with Kiyoshi Kuromiya, adjuvant)
Fuller's Earth: A Day with Bucky and the Kids, by Richard J. Brenneman
Grunch of Giants,[14] by R. Buckminster Fuller
Other books by or about R. Buckminster Fuller (various video- and audio-
    tapes are also available)[15]

TOPIC OUTLINE
    A. Introduction
        Context
        Biographical information
        Fuller's metaphysics and their historical antecedents
        Fuller's differentiation of brain and mind
        "Reform the environment, not the humans"[16]
        Make a world that works for everyone, not just a few
        Options for humanity's success
        Synergetics (energetic-synergetic geometry): the coordinate system of
            nature, the "geometry of thinking"[17]
        Humans' "critical path"
    B. "Education for comprehensivity";[18] whole-to-parts orientation
    C. Generalized principles (e.g., synergy, ephemeralization [doing more
        with less], precession,[19] eternally regenerative universe, etc.)
    D. Fuller's artifacts and strategies: practical applications of holistic
        principles
        Comprehensive Anticipatory Design Science
        Geodesic domes; Fuller's philosophy of shelter in general
        Other Fuller designs and his philosophy about them
            Dymaxion™[20] House, Dymaxion Car, Dymaxion Bathroom,
            "tensegrity" (Fuller's word for "tensional integrity" referring to
            construction based on tension, such as that used in the
            Dymaxion House, instead of the usual compression),[21] octet
            truss, etc.
        Related topics: "gestation rate" (lag between an invention and its
            general use); Buckminsterfullerene; other holistic designers
    E. Spaceship Earth
        The Fuller Projection (Dymaxion Sky-Ocean World Map)
        The Geoscope
    F. World Game
        Introduction and description
        World Game Institute
        The role of computers
        Definition of wealth: Fuller's views on economics, acceleration of
            ephemeralization, energy strategies, etc.
        Converting technology from weaponry to "livingry"
        Nationalism and politics; Fuller's views on government
    G. Invisible reality
    H. Intuition

I. Education
   Conditioned and misconditioned reflexes
   Self-education and its importance
      Global issues, culture, history, geometry, design science
   Fuller's philosophy of education[22]
      Central features
      Fundamental goal of education
      Objectives of the school
      General nature of the child as learner
      Administration and control
      General nature of the curriculum
      Instructional methods and evaluation procedures (e.g., Fuller's essay "Mistake Mystique")[23]
      Classroom harmony
      Post-secondary education and lifelong learning
   Modelability
   The intersection of science and art
   Fuller and Tao
J. Integrity
K. Fuller's philosophy compared and contrasted to that of others (Eastern and Western, historical and contemporary); evaluating criticisms of Fuller
L. Buckminster Fuller Institute and other resources
M. Fuller's legacy; implications of his work

Selected Readings

The following publications explore various aspects of the holistic paradigm and provide ample material for an intensive course on the "subject" of wholeness. Many other resources could appear on such a list. Due to the nature of holism, the categories overlap and are meant to be general guidelines only. If any of these books cannot be found at the library or book store, they can be obtained through the Interlibrary Loan System or through used/out-of-print book stores on the World Wide Web. Although reading can provide a conceptual base, awakening to wholeness often occurs through experiential means such as meditation, contemplation, and service.

Environment

Against the Grain: Biotechnology and the Corporate Takeover of Your Food, by Marc Lappé and Britt Bailey (Common Courage Press, 1998)

Betrayal of Science and Reason: How Anti-Environmental Rhetoric Threatens Our Future, by Paul R. Ehrlich and Anne H. Ehrlich (Island Press, 1996)

Censored 2000: The Year's Top 25 Censored Stories, by Peter Phillips and Project Censored (Seven Stories Press, 2000). Updated editions of this book are published yearly.

Chemical Deception: The Toxic Threat to Health and the Environment, by Marc Lappé (Sierra Club Books, 1991)

The Diversity of Life, new ed., by Edward O. Wilson (1992; rpt. W. W. Norton, 1999)

Earth Odyssey: Around the World in Search of Our Environmental Future, by Mark Hertsgaard (Broadway Books, 1998)

Ecological Literacy: Education and the Transition to a Postmodern World, by David W. Orr (State University of New York Press, 1992)

The Heat Is On: The High Stakes Battle over Earth's Threatened Climate, by Ross Gelbspan (Addison-Wesley, 1997)

Imperiled Planet: Restoring Our Endangered Ecosystems, by Edward Goldsmith et al. (MIT Press, 1990)

Ishmael: An Adventure of the Mind and Spirit, by Daniel Quinn (Bantam/Turner, 1992)

It's a Matter of Survival, by Anita Gordon and David Suzuki (Harvard University Press, 1991)

Nuclear Madness: What You Can Do, rev. ed., by Helen Caldicott, M.D. (W. W. Norton, 1994)

Overshoot: The Ecological Basis of Revolutionary Change, by William R. Catton, Jr. (1980; rpt. University of Illinois Press, 1982)

Scorched Earth: The Military's Assault on the Environment, by William Thomas (New Society Publishers, 1995)

Stolen Harvest: The Hijacking of the Global Food Supply, by Vandana Shiva (South End Press, 2000)

The War against the Greens: The "Wise-Use" Movement, the New Right, and Anti-Environmental Violence, by David Helvarg (Sierra Club Books, 1994)

Education

The Common Vision: Parenting and Educating for Wholeness, by David Marshak (Peter Lang, 1997)

Education and the Significance of Life, by J. Krishnamurti (1953; rpt. HarperSanFrancisco, 1981)

Education and the Soul: Toward a Spiritual Curriculum, by John P. Miller (State University of New York Press, 1999)

Education, Information, and Transformation: Essays on Learning and Thinking, edited by Jeffrey Kane (Merrill/Prentice Hall, 1999)

The Great Work: Our Way into the Future, by Thomas Berry (Bell Tower, 1999)

Natural Learning Rhythms: How and When Children Learn, by Josette and Sambhava Luvmour (Celestial Arts, 1993)

New Directions in Education: Selections from Holistic Education Review, edited by Ron Miller (Holistic Education Press, 1991)

Tomorrow's Children: A Blueprint for Partnership Education in the 21st Century, by Riane Eisler (Westview Press, 2000)

Transformative Learning: Educational Vision for the 21st Century, by Edmund O'Sullivan (University of Toronto/Zed Books, 1999)

The Universal Schoolhouse: Spiritual Awakening through Education, by James Moffett (Jossey-Bass, 1994)

What Are Schools For? Holistic Education in American Culture, 3d rev. ed., by Ron Miller (1990; rpt. Holistic Education Press, 1997)

Paradigm Shift / Science / Agriculture

Beyond Civilization: Humanity's Next Great Adventure, by Daniel Quinn (Harmony Books, 1999)

The Chalice and the Blade: Our History, Our Future, by Riane Eisler (Harper & Row, 1987)

Design Outlaws on the Ecological Frontier, edited by Chris Zelov and Phil Cousineau (Knossus Publishing, 1997)

Dialogues with Scientists and Sages: The Search for Unity, by Renée Weber (Routledge & Kegan Paul, 1986)

Gaia: The Human Journey from Chaos to Cosmos, by Elisabet Sahtouris (Pocket Books, 1989)

Lifting the Veil: The Feminine Face of Science, by Linda Jean Shepherd (Shambhala, 1993)

The Lives of a Cell: Notes of a Biology Watcher, by Lewis Thomas (Bantam, 1975)

The Natural Way of Farming: The Theory and Practice of Green Philosophy, by Masanobu Fukuoka, translated by Frederic P. Metreaud (Japan Publications, 1985)

The New Biology: Discovering the Wisdom in Nature, by Robert Augros and George Stanciu (Shambhala, New Science Library, 1988)

The Road Back to Nature: Regaining the Paradise Lost, by Masanobu Fukuoka, translated by Frederic P. Metreaud (Japan Publications, 1987)

The Secret Life of Plants, by Peter Tompkins and Christopher Bird (Harper & Row, 1973)

Secrets of the Soil, by Peter Tompkins and Christopher Bird (Harper & Row, 1989)

Seven Experiments That Could Change the World: A Do-It-Yourself Guide to Revolutionary Science, by Rupert Sheldrake (Riverhead Books, 1995)

The Structure of Scientific Revolutions, 2d ed., by Thomas S. Kuhn (1962; rpt. University of Chicago Press, 1970)

Tao of Chaos: Merging East and West, by Katya Walter (Kairos Center, 1994)

The Turning Point: Science, Society, and the Rising Culture, by Fritjof Capra (Simon and Schuster, 1982)

The Web of Life: A New Scientific Understanding of Living Systems, by Fritjof Capra (Anchor Books/Doubleday, 1996)

Wholeness and the Implicate Order, by David Bohm (Routledge & Kegan Paul, 1980)

The Wholeness of Nature: Goethe's Way toward a Science of Conscious Participation in Nature, by Henri Bortoft (Lindisfarne Press, 1996)

Buckminster Fuller

BuckyWorks: Buckminster Fuller's Ideas for Today, by J. Baldwin (John Wiley & Sons, 1996)

Cosmography: A Posthumous Scenario for the Future of Humanity, by R. Buckminster Fuller with Kiyoshi Kuromiya, adjuvant (Macmillan Publishing, 1992)

Critical Path, by R. Buckminster Fuller with Kiyoshi Kuromiya, adjuvant (St. Martin's Press, 1981)

"Education for Comprehensivity," by R. Buckminster Fuller, in *Approaching the Benign Environment: The Franklin Lectures in the Sciences and Humanities,* edited by Taylor Littleton (University of Alabama Press, 1970)

A Fuller Explanation: The Synergetic Geometry of R. Buckminster Fuller, by Amy C. Edmondson (Birkhauser Boston, 1987)

Fuller's Earth: A Day with Bucky and the Kids, by Richard J. Brenneman (St. Martin's Press, 1984)

Grunch of Giants,[1] by R. Buckminster Fuller (St. Martin's Press, 1983)

Humans in Universe, by R. Buckminster Fuller and Anwar Dil (Mouton, 1983)

Intuition, by R. Buckminster Fuller (1972; rpt. Impact Publishers, 1983)

Operating Manual for Spaceship Earth, by R. Buckminster Fuller (1963; rpt. E. P. Dutton, 1978)

R. Buckminster Fuller on Education, edited by Peter H. Wagschal and Robert D. Kahn (University of Massachusetts Press, 1979)

Utopia or Oblivion: The Prospects for Humanity, by R. Buckminster Fuller (Overlook Press, 1969)

Your Private Sky: R. Buckminster Fuller, The Art of Design Science, edited by Joachim Krausse and Claude Lichtenstein (Lars Müller Publishers, 1999)

Philosophy / Spirituality / Poetry

Care of the Soul: A Guide for Cultivating Depth and Sacredness in Everyday Life, by Thomas Moore (HarperCollins, 1992)

The Collected Poems and Plays, by Rabindranath Tagore (1913; rpt. Macmillan Publishing Co./Collier Books, 1993)

The Dhammapada: The Sayings of the Buddha, a new rendering by Thomas Byrom, photography by Sandra Weiner (Alfred A. Knopf, 1976)

The Enlightened Heart: An Anthology of Sacred Poetry, edited by Stephen Mitchell (Harper & Row, 1989)

A Guide for the Perplexed, by E. F. Schumacher (Harper & Row, 1977)

hsin hsin ming (verses on the faith-mind), by Sengtsan, translated by Richard B. Clarke (White Pine Press, 1984)[2]

The Illuminated Rumi, translations and commentary by Coleman Barks, illuminations by Michael Green (Broadway Books, 1997)

Joseph Campbell and The Power of Myth: with Bill Moyers, produced by Apostrophe S Productions in association with Alvin H. Perlmutter, Inc. and Public Affairs Television, Inc., 1988. (This program consists of a series of six interviews available on both video and audio cassette.)

The Kabir Book: Forty-Four of the Ecstatic Poems of Kabir, versions by Robert Bly (Beacon Press, 1977)

Meditations, by J. Krishnamurti (Harper & Row, 1979)

Open Secret: Versions of Rumi, by John Moyne and Coleman Barks (Threshold Books, 1984)

The Perennial Philosophy, by Aldous Huxley (1944; rpt. Harper & Row, 1970)

The Prophet, by Kahlil Gibran (1923; rpt. Alfred A. Knopf, 1963)

Tao Te Ching, by Lao-tzu,[3] translated by Gia-fu Feng and Jane English (1972; rpt. Random House, 1997)

Tao: The Watercourse Way, by Alan Watts with the collaboration of Al Chung-liang Huang (Pantheon Books, 1975)

The Way of Chuang Tzu, by Thomas Merton (New Directions, 1969)

The Zen Teaching of Huang Po: On the Transmission of Mind, translated by John Blofeld (Grove Press, 1958)

Economics / Government / Sociology / History / Community

Beyond Globalization: Shaping a Sustainable Global Economy, by Hazel Henderson for the New Economics Foundation in association with Focus on the Global South (Kumarian Press, 1999)

The Book of Leadership and Strategy: Lessons of the Chinese Masters, translated by Thomas Cleary (Shambhala, 1992)

Building a Win-Win World: Life beyond Global Economic Warfare, by Hazel Henderson (Berritt-Koehler Publishers, 1996)

Dirty Truths: Reflections on Politics, Media, Ideology, Conspiracy, Ethnic Life and Class Power, by Michael Parenti (City Lights Books, 1996)

Manufacturing Consent: The Political Economy of the Mass Media, by Edward S. Herman and Noam Chomsky (Pantheon Books, 1988)

Necessary Illusions: Thought Control in Democratic Societies, by Noam Chomsky (South End Press, 1989)

Paradigms in Progress: Life Beyond Economics, by Hazel Henderson (Berritt-Koehler Publishers, 1995)

A People's History of the United States, by Howard Zinn (Harper & Row, 1980)

The Politics of the Solar Age: Alternatives to Economics, by Hazel Henderson (Anchor Press/Doubleday, 1981)

Profit over People: Neoliberalism and Global Order, by Noam Chomsky (Seven Stories Press, 1999)

The Prosperous Few and the Restless Many, by Noam Chomsky (Odonian Press, 1993)

The Quickening of America: Rebuilding Our Nation, Remaking Our Lives, by Frances Moore Lappé and Paul Martin Du Bois (Jossey-Bass, 1994)

Small is Beautiful: Economics as if People Mattered, by E. F. Schumacher (1973; rpt. Harper & Row, 1975)

Trilateralism: The Trilateral Commission and Elite Planning for World Management, edited by Holly Sklar (South End Press, 1980)

What Uncle Sam Really Wants, by Noam Chomsky (Odonian Press, 1992)

World Hunger: Twelve Myths, by Frances Moore Lappé and Joseph Collins (Grove Press, 1986)

Year 501: The Conquest Continues, by Noam Chomsky (South End Press, 1993)

Holistic Health

Diet for a New America, by John Robbins (1987; rpt. HJ Kramer, 1998)

Eating Well for Optimum Health: The Essential Guide to Food, Diet, and Nutrition, by Andrew Weil, M.D. (Alfred A. Knopf, 2000)

Eight Weeks to Optimum Health: A Proven Program for Taking Full Advantage of Your Body's Natural Healing Power, by Andrew Weil, M.D. (Alfred A. Knopf, 1998)

The Good Life: Helen and Scott Nearing's Sixty Years of Self-Sufficient Living, by Helen Nearing and Scott Nearing (1954, 1979; rpt. Shocken Books, 1989)

Health at the Crossroads: Exploring the Conflict Between Natural Healing and Conventional Medicine, by Dean Black (Tapestry Press, 1988)

May All Be Fed: Diet for a New World, Including Recipes by Jia Patton and Friends, by John Robbins (William Morrow, 1992)

Reclaiming Our Health: Exploding the Medical Myth and Embracing the Source of True Healing, by John Robbins (HJ Kramer, 1996)

Spontaneous Healing: How to Discover and Enhance Your Body's Natural Ability to Maintain and Heal Itself, by Andrew Weil, M.D. (Alfred A. Knopf, 1995)

Appendix C
Additional Resources

The following organizations are concerned with practical applications of holistic principles. These sources lead to many more.

Buckminster Fuller Institute
111 N. Main Street
Sebastopol, CA 95472
phone: (800) 967-6277
(707) 824-2242
fax: (707) 824-2243
www.bfi.org

Earth Island Institute
300 Broadway, Suite 28
San Francisco, CA 94133
phone: (415) 788-3666
fax: (415) 788-7324
www.earthisland.org

Foundation for Education Renewal/
   Holistic Education Press
P.O. Box 328
Brandon, VT 05733-0328
phone and fax: (802) 247-8312
www.PathsOfLearning.net
www.great-ideas.org

Institute for Local Self-Reliance
1313 5th Street SE
Minneapolis, MN 55414
phone: (612) 379-3815
fax: (612) 379-3920
www.ilsr.org

Ocean Arks International,
   Ecological Solutions for the
   21st Century
176 Battery Street
Burlington, VT 05401
phone: (802) 860-0011
fax: (802) 860-0022
www.oceanarks.org

Rocky Mountain Institute
1739 Snowmass Creek Road
Snowmass, CO 81654-9199
phone: (970) 927-3851
fax: (970) 927-3420
www.rmi.org

World Game Institute
3215 Race Street
Philadelphia, PA 19104
phone: (215) 387-0220
fax: (215) 387-3009
www.worldgame.org

Appendix D
Some Holistic Education Activities

For educators:

1. Select from books listed in appendix B (and other sources), investigating compelling themes that surface while reading. Create ways to integrate holistic education into the existing curriculum. Emphasize objective rationales for holism, which will help to refute charges that a new type of "religion" is being introduced into schools. Stress that holism is not another "ism," but a practical tool to help discern among the numerous "isms" presented throughout life.

2. With students, identify various manifestations of the features of holism presented in chapter one with respect to one or more of the following areas: the arts, the sciences, health and nutrition, environmental studies, spirituality, education, economics, agriculture, government, athletics, etc.

3. Create for students at each grade, levels K-12, a year-long course focusing on wholeness as a "subject." Develop a list of appropriate multimedia holistic resources for distribution to students and parents.

4. Invite high school and university students to create presentations of books selected from appendix B (and other sources), each presenter facilitating a discussion of the major ideas covered.

5. Establish periods for communing in stillness with the inexpressible mysteries of the whole. Consider various locations outside the classroom, including those suggested by students.

6. Establish monthly faculty reading/discussion groups based on the "subject" of wholeness, encouraging parents to attend. Ask the "big questions" relevant to humanity as a whole and to each individual. Develop practical applications and undertake shared holistic projects.

For families, couples, singles, retirees, groups (i.e., everyone):

1. Ask those involved to suggest holistic activities in which all can participate (keeping in mind that every activity is holistic when wholeness is the orientation). Examples include excursions in nature and field trips to organic farms or alternative energy installations; attendance at workshops and lectures; discussions of educational videos and all sorts of books; participation in projects that benefit the environment; and taking part in family or group yoga, music, and dance.

2. Create a musical ensemble and play together regularly. A simple format is a drumming circle/percussion group using inexpensive hand-held instruments such as hand drums, wood blocks, triangles, small cymbals, shakers, rattles, bells, etc.[1] Emphasize sensitivity and simplicity. Experience the truth of the statement "the whole is greater than the sum of its parts."

3. Create neighborhood art and garden projects. Spend time with and perhaps mentor youth and others, especially those neglected by society.

4. Present the "subject" of wholeness to a church, synagogue, mosque, etc. Facilitate discussion of how wholeness relates to that group's original teachings.

APPENDIX E

Interdependence of World Problems

by Fritjof Capra

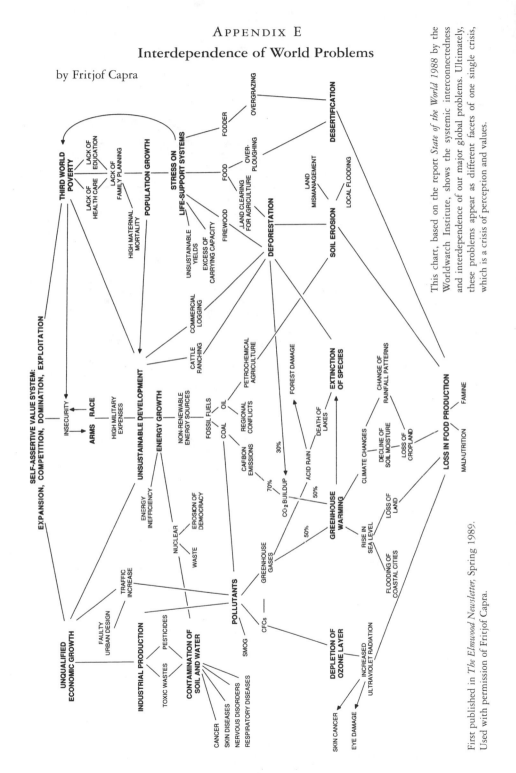

This chart, based on the report *State of the World 1988* by the Worldwatch Institute, shows the systemic interconnectedness and interdependence of our major global problems. Ultimately, these problems appear as different facets of one single crisis, which is a crisis of perception and values.

First published in *The Elmwood Newsletter*, Spring 1989. Used with permission of Fritjof Capra.

World Game Institute's "What the World Wants"

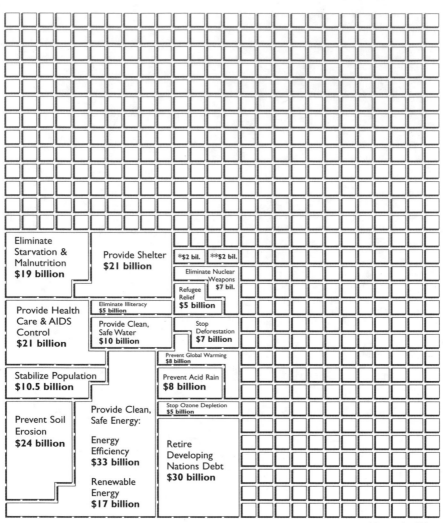

Eliminate Starvation & Malnutrition $19 billion

Provide Shelter $21 billion

*$2 bil. **$2 bil.

Eliminate Nuclear Weapons $7 bil.

Refugee Relief $5 billion

Provide Health Care & AIDS Control $21 billion

Eliminate Illiteracy $5 billion

Provide Clean, Safe Water $10 billion

Stop Deforestation $7 billion

Prevent Global Warming $8 billion

Stabilize Population $10.5 billion

Prevent Acid Rain $8 billion

Stop Ozone Depletion $5 billion

Prevent Soil Erosion $24 billion

Provide Clean, Safe Energy:

Energy Efficiency $33 billion

Renewable Energy $17 billion

Retire Developing Nations Debt $30 billion

* Remove Land Mines
** Build Democracy

AND HOW TO PAY FOR IT USING MILITARY EXPENDITURES

Above are annual costs of various global programs for solving the major human needs and environmental problems facing humanity. Each program notes the cost of accomplishing its goal throughout the world. Their combined total cost is approximately 30% of the world's total annual military expenditures.

Total chart represents annual world military expenditures: $780 billion

☐ = $1 billion

◼ = Amount that was needed to eradicate smallpox from the world (accomplished in 1978): $300 million

What the World Wants (cont.)
This chart seeks to make the point that what the world needs to solve the major systemic problems confronting humanity is both available and affordable. Clearly, representing a problem as complex and large as the global food situation, for example, with just a small part of a single graph, is approximate at best. The following explanations of the chart's various components are not intended as complete or detailed plans, but rather as very broad brush strokes intended to give the overall direction, scope, and strategy. The paper, "What the World Wants Project," goes into more detail. It is available from the World Game Institute. (References listed on the next page contain supporting documentation, further explication, and related information.)

STRATEGY 1. ELIMINATE STARVATION AND MALNOURISHMENT/FEEDING HUMANITY: $19 billion per year for ten years, allocated as follows: $2 billion per year for an International Famine Relief Agency—spent on international grain reserve and emergency famine relief; $10 billion per year spent on farmer education through vastly expanded in-country extension services that teach/demonstrate sustainable agriculture, use of local fertilizer sources, pest and soil management techniques, and post harvest preservation, and which provide clear market incentives for increased local production; $7 billion per year for indigenous fertilizer development. Educational resources of Strategy 10 are coupled with this strategy. Closely linked with #'s 2, 3, 4, 9, 10. *Cost: 55% of what the U.S. spends on weight loss per year.*

STRATEGY 2A. PROVIDE HEALTH CARE FOR ALL: $15 billion per year for ten years spent on providing primary health care through community health workers to all areas in the world that do not have access to health care. Closely linked with #'s 1, 3, 4, 5, 9.

STRATEGY 2B. PROVIDE SPECIAL CHILD HEALTH CARE: Within the $15 billion, $2.5 billion per year spent on: a) providing vitamin A to children who lack it in their diet, thereby preventing blindness in 250,000 children/year; b) providing oral rehydration therapy for children with severe diarrhea; and c) immunizing 1 billion children in the developing world against measles, tuberculosis, diphtheria, whooping cough, polio, and tetanus, thereby preventing the death of 6 to 7 million children/year.

STRATEGY 2C. IODINE DEFICIENCY PROGRAM: $40 million per year for iodine addition to table salt to eliminate iodine deficiency, thereby reducing the 566 million people who suffer from goiter and not adding to the 3 million who suffer from overt cretinism.

STRATEGY 2D. AIDS PREVENTION AND CONTROL PROGRAM: $6 billion per year allocated as follows: $3 billion per year for a global AIDS prevention education program; $2 billion per year for providing multiple drug therapy to AIDS patients in the developing world; $1 billion per year for research and development for an AIDS vaccine or cure. *Costs for all Health Care Strategies: 16% of what the U.S. spends on alcohol and tobacco per year.*

STRATEGY 3. ELIMINATE INADEQUATE HOUSING AND HOMELESSNESS: $21 billion per year for ten years spent on making available materials, tools, and techniques to people without adequate housing. Closely linked with #'s 1, 4, 5, 9. *Cost: amount the U.S. spends on golf every 16 months.*

STRATEGY 4. PROVIDE CLEAN AND ABUNDANT WATER: $10 billion per year for ten years spent on making available materials, tools, and training needed to build and maintain the needed wells, water and sewage pipes, sanitation facilities, and water purifying systems. Closely related to #'s 1, 2, 3, 9. *Cost: 1% of what the world spends on illegal drugs per year.*

STRATEGY 5. ELIMINATE ILLITERACY: $5 billion per year for ten years; $2 billion spent on a system of 10 to 12 communication satellites and their launching; $2 billion spent on ten million televisions, satellite dish receivers, and photovoltaic/battery units for power—all placed in village schools and throughout other high illiteracy areas; the rest (90% of funds) spent on culturally appropriate literacy programming and maintenance of system. Closely related to #'s 1, 2, 3, 4, 9, 10, 11. *Cost: 5% of the cost of the Gulf War; what the U.S. spends on video games in 14 months.*

STRATEGY 6. INCREASE ENERGY EFFICIENCY: $33 billion per year for ten years spent on increasing car fleet mileage to over 50 mpg, plus increasing appliance, industrial processes, and household energy and materials use to state of the art. Closely linked with #'s 7, 8, 12, 13, 14. *Cost: 13% of what U.S. teenagers spend per year.*

STRATEGY 7. INCREASE RENEWABLE ENERGY: $17 billion per year for ten years spent on tax and other incentives for installation of renewable energy devices, graduated ten-year phaseout of subsidies to fossil and nuclear fuels, research and development into more advanced renewable energy-harnessing devices. Closely linked with #'s 6, 8, 11 12, 13, 14. *Cost: 13% of the amount of current subsidies to electricity prices in the developing world.*

STRATEGY 8. DEBT MANAGEMENT: $30 billion per year for ten years spent on retiring $500 billion or more of current debt discounted to 50% face value. Not only helps developing countries get out of debt, but helps banks stay solvent and furthers international trade. Closely linked with #'s 1, 6, 7, 10, 11, 14. *Cost: 3.8% of the world's annual military expenditures.*

STRATEGY 9. STABILIZE POPULATION: $10.5 billion per year for ten years spent on making birth control universally available. Closely linked with #'s 1, 2, 3, 4, 5. *Cost: 1.3% of the world's annual military expenditures.*

STRATEGY 10. PRESERVING CROPLAND: $24 billion per year for ten years spent on converting one-tenth of the world's most vulnerable cropland that is simultaneously the most susceptible to erosion, the location of most severe erosion, and the land that is no longer able to sustain agriculture, to pasture or woodland; and conserving and regenerating the topsoil on remaining lands through sustainable farming techniques. Both accomplished through a combination of government regulation and incentive programs that remove the most vulnerable lands from crop production; and by farmer education through vastly expanded in-country extension services that teach/demonstrate sustainable agriculture and soil management techniques. Closely linked to #1. *Cost: $3 billion less than the annual cost of U.S. farmland loss; half the amount of price subsidies given to U.S. and European farmers.*

STRATEGY 11. REVERSE DEFORESTATION: $7 billion per year for ten years spent on reforesting 150 million hectares needed to sustain ecological, fuelwood, and wood products needs. If the planting were done by local villagers, costs would be $400 per hectare, including seedling costs. Additional costs for legislation, financial incentives, enforcement of rainforest protection. Closely linked with #'s 10, 11. *Cost: 0.9% of the world's annual military expenditures.*

STRATEGY 12. REVERSE OZONE DEPLETION: $5 billion per year for twenty years spent on phasing in substitutes for CFC-20, CFC taxes, incentives for further research and development. Closely linked with #14. *Cost: 3.7% of U.S. government subsidies to energy, timber, construction, financial services, and advertising industries.*

STRATEGY 13. STOP ACID RAIN: $8 billion per year for ten years spent on combination of tax incentives, government regulation, and direct assistance programs that place pollution control devices (electrostatic precipitators, etc.) on all industrial users of coal, increase efficiency of industrial processes, cars, and appliances. Closely linked to #'s 6, 7, 11, 14. *Cost: about 1% of the world's annual military expenditures.*

STRATEGY 14. REVERSE GLOBAL WARMING: $8 billion per year for twenty years spent on reducing carbon dioxide, methane, and CFC release into the atmosphere through a combination of international accords, carbon taxes, increases in energy efficiency in industry, transportation, and household, decreases in fossil fuel use, increases in renewable energy use and reforestation. Closely linked with #'s 6, 7, 11, 13. *Cost: 17% of what the insurance industry paid out in the 1990s for weather-related damage; 1% of the world's annual military expenditures.*

STRATEGY 15. REMOVAL OF LANDMINES: $2 billion per year for ten years spent on setting up cottage industries in each of the 64 countries that have landmines planted in their soils. Participants are intensively trained in the safe removal of landmines; compensation set at more than a day's wage for each removed mine in each respective country. Closely linked with #'s 2, 16, 17, 18. *Cost: less than the cost of a single B-2 bomber; less than one-half of what the U.S. spends on perfume each year.*

STRATEGY 16. REFUGEE RELIEF: $5 billion per year for ten years spent on an international Refugee Relief Agency that guarantees the safety of refugees and coordinates the delivery of food, shelter, health care, and education. Closely linked with #'s 1, 2, 3, 4, 15, 18. *Cost: 20% of the amount of arms sales to developing countries.*

STRATEGY 17. ELIMINATING NUCLEAR WEAPONS: $7 billion per year for ten years spent on dismantling all the world's nuclear weapons and processing the plutonium and enriched uranium in nuclear reactors that produce power and render the radioactive materials into nonweapons-grade material. Closely linked with #'s 15, 16, 18. *Cost: 25% of what is spent each year on private "security": private guards, weapons detectors, video surveillance, etc.*

STRATEGY 18. BUILDING DEMOCRACY: $2 billion per year for ten years spent on the following programs: an International Democratic Election Fund that would help finance voter education and multi-party elections in countries making the transition to democracy; a Global Polling Program that would ascertain what people from all over the world think and feel about key *global* issues; and a Global Problem-Solving Simulation Tool that would enable anyone with access to the Internet to propose, develop, and test strategies for solving real-world problems. Closely linked with #'s 5, 15, 16, 17. *Cost for all three programs: less than one B-2 bomber; 0.025% of the world's annual military expenditures.*

MAJOR REFERENCES: UNDP, *Human Development Report 1996* (New York: Oxford University Press, 1996); UNICEF, *State of the World's Children 1996, 1995, 1994* (New York: Oxford University Press, 1996, 1995, 1994); UNICEF, *Giving Children a Future: The World Summit for Children, 29-30 September 1990* (New York: United Nations, 1990); UNHCR, *Refugees,* no. 11, 1995 (Geneva: Public Information Section of the UNHCR, 1995); The World Bank, *World Development Report 1996* (New York: Oxford University Press, 1996); World Resources Institute, *World Resources 1994-95, 1992-93* (New York: Oxford University Press, 1995, 1993); Lester R. Brown et al., *Vital Signs 1996,* and *State of the World, 1988* through *1996* (New York: W. W. Norton, 1988-1996); Medard Gabel, with the World Game Laboratory, *Energy, Earth, and Everyone: A Global Strategy for Spaceship Earth* (San Francisco: Straight Arrow Books, 1975), and *Ho-Ping—Food for Everyone* (New York: Anchor Press/Doubleday, 1979).

NOTES

Epigraph

The Illuminated Rumi, translations and commentary by Coleman Barks, illuminations by Michael Green (New York: Broadway Books, 1997), p. 31. Jelaluddin
Rumi (1207-1273) was a Persian mystic and poet.

Chapter 1

Epigraph: R. Buckminster Fuller with Jerome Agel and Quentin Fiore, *I Seem to
Be a Verb* (New York: Bantam, 1970), p. 6 and front cover. See also R. Buckminster
Fuller, *Operating Manual for Spaceship Earth* (1963; rpt. New York: E. P. Dutton,
1978), p. 52.

1. This paragraph is adapted from David W. Orr, *Ecological Literacy: Education and the
Transition to a Postmodern World* (Albany: State University of New York Press,
1992), p. 3. The statistics have been updated from the following sources:

   For "17 million tons of carbon," see Lester R. Brown et al., *Vital Signs 2000:
The Environmental Trends That Are Shaping Our Future,* ed. Linda Starke (New York:
W. W. Norton & Co., 2000), p. 67 (this is a preliminary figure for 1999).

   For "169 square miles of forest (net)," see Lester R. Brown et al., *Vital Signs
1998: The Environmental Trends That Are Shaping Our Future,* ed. Linda Starke (New
York: W. W. Norton & Co., 1998), p. 124. Edward O. Wilson notes with regard
to the *rain* forests that an area about half the size of Florida is being lost each year
("Biodiversity: Vanishing before Our Eyes," *Time* 155 [April-May 2000, special
edition]: 30).

   For "42 square miles of agriculturally useful drylands," see "What on Earth?
A Weekly Look at Trends, People and Events around the World," *Washington Post,*
22 Aug. 1998 (source cited: International Fund for Agricultural Development,
USDA).

   For "more than 74 species," see Edward O. Wilson, *The Diversity of Life,* new
ed. (1992; rpt. New York: W. W. Norton & Co., 1999), p. 280 (this figure considers "only species being lost by reduction in forest area . . . [and does] not
include overharvesting or invasion by alien organisms").

   For "more than three million tons of topsoil," see Lester R. Brown et al., *Vital
Signs 1995: The Trends That Are Shaping Our Future,* ed. Linda Starke (New York:
W. W. Norton & Co., 1995), p. 118 (where it states that the U.S. is one of the only
countries that closely monitors loss of topsoil).

   "435 tons of chlorofluorocarbons" is from a 16 Dec. 1999 conversation with
Molly O'Meara Sheehan (research associate, Worldwatch Institute, Washington,
D.C.), who wrote the chapter on CFC production in *Vital Signs 1998* cited above.
According to Sheehan, these are the most recent statistics available. She notes in
Vital Signs 1998: "Although CFCs are on the decline, other ozone-depleting com-
pounds are not" (p. 70).

   For "the human population will increase," see *Vital Signs 2000,* p. 99 (this is
a preliminary figure for 1999).

2. See *Intersun: The Global UV Project,* 29 Oct. 1998, World Health Organization, 17
July 2000 <www.who.int/peh-uv/>; see also "Estimating UV's Human Cancer
Risk: Skin Cancer Risk Posed by Ultraviolet Light Increases as Stratospheric
Ozone Declines," *Science News* 146 (15 Oct. 1994): 255.

3. See "The Global Environmental Crisis: Causes, Connections, and Solutions" (brief-
ing paper), Union of Concerned Scientists, Cambridge, Mass., April 1994, p. 1;
Mark Dowie, "A Sky Full of Holes: Why the Ozone Layer Is Torn Worse Than
Ever," *Nation* 263 (8 July 1996): 11-16; and Jim Scanlon, "Silenced Science:
Arctic Ozone Loss," *Earth Island Journal* 13 (Fall 1998): 23.

4. "The Global Environmental Crisis" (as per note 3), p. 2. The Union of Concerned Scientists is described in note 19. See also *Climate Change 1995: The Science of Climate Change,* ed. J. T. Houghton et al. (Cambridge University Press, 1996):

> If carbon dioxide emissions were maintained at near current (1994) levels, they would lead to a nearly constant rate of increase in atmospheric concentrations for at least two centuries, reaching about 500 ppmv [parts per million by volume] (approaching twice the pre-industrial concentration of 280 ppmv) by the end of the 21st century. (p. 3)

5. See Dowie (as per note 3), and Scanlon (as per note 3). Dowie writes that, according to Dr. Jerry Mahlman, director of the National Oceanic and Atmospheric Administration's Geophysical Fluid Dynamics Laboratory in Princeton, New Jersey,

> Greenhouse gases trap warm air in the atmospheric layer below the stratosphere, and this causes the stratosphere itself to cool. Polar ice clouds then form in the stratosphere, where ice crystals catalyze ozone depletion. A feedback loop ensues, as the ozone depletion caused by global warming allows more ultraviolet radiation to reach the earth. These rays create more greenhouse gases and additional global warming. That leads to more ozone depletion. The cycle continues, and the loop expands. (p. 16)

6. See "Vanishing Forests, Disappearing Clouds," *Earth Island Journal* 7 (Fall 1992): 27. See also appendix E.
7. See Norman Myers, *The Primary Source: Tropical Forests and Our Future* (1985; rpt. New York: W. W. Norton & Co., 1992), p. 50; Edward O. Wilson, "Biophilia and the Conservation Ethic," in *The Biophilia Hypothesis,* ed. Stephen R. Kellert and Edward O. Wilson (Washington, D.C.: Island Press, 1993), p. 36; and Wilson, *The Diversity of Life* (as per note 1), pp. 276-77.
8. Wilson, *The Diversity of Life,* p. 12.
9. See R. T. Watson, V. H. Heywood, et al., *Global Biodiversity Assessment: Summary for Policy-Makers* (Cambridge: Cambridge University Press for the United Nations Environment Programme, 1995), p. 24. The authors also note:

> Projections of impending extinctions due to habitat loss can be made using the empirical relationship between the number of species and the area of a habitat, derived from island biogeography. When applied to tropical forests, published estimates of the number of species that will eventually become extinct or committed to extinction due to projected forest loss over the next 25 years or so range from 2% to 25% in the various groups examined (mainly plants and birds): this would be equivalent to 1,000 to 10,000 times the expected background rate. (p. 2)

See also p. 25.
10. See *Global Biodiversity Assessment,* exec. ed. Vernon H. Heywood (Cambridge, Eng.: Cambridge University Press for the United Nations Environment Programme, 1995), chapter 11 and pp. 240-45.
11. Wilson, *The Diversity of Life* (as per note 1), p. 32. Wilson notes that recently some paleontologists have interpreted the mass-extinction event in the early Cambrian period to be of the same magnitude as the other five, which would mean that the world is now in the midst of the seventh, not the sixth, such event (5 June 2000 conversation with the author; see also "Biodiversity: Vanishing before Our Eyes" [as per note 1]: 30).
12. Wilson, *The Diversity of Life,* p. ix.
13. Adapted from Norman R. Farnsworth, "Screening Plants for New Medicines," in *Biodiversity,* ed. E. O. Wilson (Washington, D.C.: National Academy Press, 1988), pp. 83 and 91; and paraphrased from Wilson, *The Diversity of Life,* p. 283 and 285. Wilson writes, "Yet these materials are only a tiny fraction of the multitude available. [For example,] fewer than 3 percent of the flowering plants of the world, about 5,000 of the 220,000 species, have been examined for alkaloids, and then in limited and haphazard fashion" (p. 285). See also Mark J. Plotkin, *Medicine Quest:*

In Search of Nature's Healing Secrets (New York: Penguin Putnam, 2000), pp. 22 and 26. Plotkin writes, "Almost half of all the best-selling pharmaceuticals in the early 1990s were natural products or their derivatives" (p. 26).

14. See Paul R. Ehrlich and Anne H. Ehrlich, *Betrayal of Science and Reason: How Anti-Environmental Rhetoric Threatens Our Future* (Washington, D.C.: Island Press, 1996), p. 153.

15. See *Chemicals in Our Community,* Fall 1998, U.S. Environmental Protection Agency Office of Pollution Prevention and Toxics, 30 Nov. 2000 <www.epa.gov/opptintr/chemcomm>.

16. See Richard Wiles et al., *Same as it ever was . . . : The Clinton Administration's 1993 Pesticide Reduction Policy in Perspective* (Washington, D.C.: Environmental Working Group, 1998), pp. 2-5. See also "How Safe Is Our Produce?" *Consumer Reports* 64 (March 1999): 28-31; and Peter Phillips and Project Censored, *Censored 2000: The Year's Top 25 Censored Stories* (New York: Seven Stories Press, 2000), pp. 67-70 ("Early Puberty Onset for Girls May Be Linked to Chemicals in the Environment and Increases in Breast Cancer").

17. See *Cancer Facts & Figures 2000* (Atlanta: American Cancer Society, 2000) pp. 1 and 11. The data source cited is DEVCAN Software, Version 4.0, Surveillance, Epidemiology, and End Results Program, 1973-1996, Division of Cancer Control and Population Sciences, National Cancer Institute, referring to 1994-1996.

18. See Fritjof Capra, *The Turning Point: Science, Society, and the Rising Culture* (New York: Simon and Schuster, 1982), pp. 245 and 246. Capra states:

> The half-life of plutonium (PU-239)—the time after which one-half of a given quantity has decayed—is 24,400 years. This means that if one gram of plutonium is released into the environment, about one-millionth of a gram will be left after 500,000 years [which, Capra notes, is an invisible dose, but one that is still carcinogenic]. . . . This is the length of time that plutonium must be isolated from the environment. What moral right do we have to leave such a deadly legacy to thousands and thousands of generations? (pp. 245-46)

See also Helen Caldicott, M.D., *Nuclear Madness: What You Can Do,* rev. ed. (New York: W. W. Norton & Co., 1994), p. 82 (also pp. 30, 80, 134, and chapter 11); and Peter Phillips and Project Censored, *Censored 1999: The News That Didn't Make the News—The Year's Top 25 Censored Stories* (New York: Seven Stories Press, 1999), pp. 109-10 ("Russian Plutonium Lost Over Chile and Bolivia").

19. "World Scientists' Warning to Humanity" (bulletin), Union of Concerned Scientists, Cambridge, Mass., April 1993, p. 1. More than 1,670 scientists, including 104 Nobel laureates (a majority of the living recipients of the Prize in the sciences) have signed the warning. The bulletin states, "These men and women represent 71 countries, including all of the 19 largest economic powers, all of the 12 most populous nations, 12 countries in Africa, 14 in Asia, 19 in Europe, and 12 in Latin America." (The Union of Concerned Scientists is an independent nonprofit alliance of concerned citizens and scientists headquartered in Cambridge, Mass.)

20. Marilyn August (Associated Press), "Cousteau Gives Last Warning to Mankind in Upcoming Book: Humans Have 100 Years Left, At Most, Warns Memoir Published Just a Week After His Death," *Seattle Times,* 1 July 1997. This article concerns Cousteau's posthumously published autobiography, *L'homme, la pieuvre et l'orchidée* [Man, Octopus and Orchid] (Jacques-Yves Cousteau with Susan Schiefelbein, Paris: Robert Laffont, 1997). The translation of the quotation as it appeared in the article was provided by the Associated Press (the book has not yet been published in English).

21. David Helvarg, "The Greenhouse Spin: Energy Companies Try the 'Tobacco' Approach to Evidence of Global Warming," *Nation* 263 (16 Dec. 1996): 21. See also David Helvarg, *The War against the Greens: The "Wise-Use" Movement, the New Right, and Anti-Environmental Violence* (San Francisco: Sierra Club Books, 1994); Ross Gelbspan, *The Heat Is On: The High Stakes Battle over Earth's Threatened Climate* (Reading, Mass.: Addison-Wesley Publishing Co., 1997); and Ehrlich and Ehrlich (as per note 14).

22. *Climate Change 1995* (as per note 4), pp. 4, 3, 7, and 336. For a more definite conclusion, see Don Kennedy, "New Climate News," *Science* 290 (10 Nov. 2000): 1091.
23. See "The Chlorine Cover-up: An Interview with Adam Trombly," *Earth Island Journal* 7 (Fall 1992): 25-26. For an article concerning the relative advantages and disadvantages of chlorine see Ivan Amato, "Crusade to Ban Chlorine," *Garbage: The Independent Environmental Quarterly* 6 (Summer 1994): 30-39.
24. See Dowie (as per note 3). The author states:

   > [There is a distinct possibility that] whole sections of the stratosphere, separate from the Antarctic, could be pushed into a dangerous state of "nonlinearity" [according to Dr. Jerry Mahlman; see note 5]. This is a condition in which every new molecule of an ozone-harming substance destroys ozone to a greater extent than the previous molecule. "The atmosphere tends to work on a straw-that-broke-the-camel's-back model," explains Arjun Makhijani, a member of the E.P.A.'s Committee on Environmental Policy and Technology. "It tolerates pollutants up to certain critical levels or thresholds, then suddenly gives way. Crossing critical thresholds has already given us nasty surprises." (p. 15)

   See also William H. Calvin, "The Great Climate Flip-flop," *Atlantic Monthly* 281 (Jan. 1998): 47-64.
25. "The Global Environmental Crisis" (as per note 3), pp. 1-2.
26. See Roger H. Bezdek, "Environment and Economy: What's the Bottom Line?" *Environment* 35 (Sept. 1993): 7-11, 25-32; Ehrlich and Ehrlich (as per note 14), p. 181; Union of Concerned Scientists and Tellus Institute, *A Small Price to Pay: U.S. Action to Curb Global Warming Is Feasible and Affordable* (Cambridge, Mass.: Union of Concerned Scientists, July 1998); Helvarg, *The War against the Greens* (as per note 21), chapter 14; Armory B. Lovins and L. Hunter Lovins, *Climate: Making Sense and Making Money* (Old Snowmass, Colorado: Rocky Mountain Institute, 1997), which was written at the request of the President's Council on Sustainable Development; "Climate Protection for Fun and Profit: New RMI Study Strikes a Chord in High Places," *Rocky Mountain Institute Newsletter* (Fall/Winter 1997): 1-3; and Chad Hanson, "Ending Logging on National Forests: The Facts," *Earth Island Journal* 14 (Summer 1999): pullout section (the author is executive director of The John Muir Project of the Earth Island Institute). Two related articles are Robert Costanza et al., "The Value of the World's Ecosystem Services and Natural Capital," *Nature* 387 (15 May 1997): 253-60; and Stuart L. Pimm, "The Value of Everything," ibid.: 231-32.
27. Ehrlich and Ehrlich (as per note 14), pp. 185-86.
28. Ibid., p. 186.
29. See, for example, "The National Entertainment State," a series of articles in *The Nation.* Part one of the series appears in vol. 262 (3 June 1996); part two: vol. 264 (17 March 1997); part three: vol. 265 (25 Aug./1 Sept. 1997); part four: vol. 266 (8 June 1998). Mega-mergers of media companies have continued to occur since these articles were written.
30. See Phillips and Project Censored, *Censored 2000* (as per note 16). This book is listed in appendix B.
31. See *The Encyclopedia of Eastern Philosophy and Religion: Buddhism, Hinduism, Taoism, Zen,* ed. Stephan Schuhmacher and Gert Woerner (1986; rpt. Boston: Shambhala, 1989), p. 421.
32. Ibid. Appendixes E and F contain essential information pertaining to environmental restoration.
33. For excellent analyses of the environmental crisis see the books listed in the first section of appendix B. See also *Earth Island Journal,* a quarterly of international environmental news published by Earth Island Institute, San Francisco (noted in appendix C).
34. "The Global Environmental Crisis" (as per note 3), p. 1.
35. As early as 1989, the mass media featured the need to "save" Earth (see *Time* magazine cover story "Endangered Earth," 2 Jan. 1989). In 1990, the actress Meryl Streep hosted a PBS television series entitled "Race to Save the Planet." There have

been a number of similar articles and programs continuing into the present. The World Scientists' Warning to Humanity (as per note 19) is basically a plea for everyone to join this "race."

36. See Herman E. Daly, "The Steady-State Economy: Toward a Political Economy of Biophysical Equilibrium and Moral Growth," *Toward a Steady-State Economy*, ed. Herman E. Daly (San Francisco: W. H. Freeman and Co., 1973).

37. For information about how the social milieu is designed and reinforced, see books by Noam Chomsky (some of which are listed in appendix B). See also *A People's History of the United States,* by Howard Zinn; *Trilateralism: The Trilateral Commission and Elite Planning for World Management,* edited by Holly Sklar (both listed in appendix B); and books, tapes, and videos by the political analyst and media critic Michael Parenti (available from People's Video/Audio, P.O. Box 99514, Seattle, WA 98199 <www.michaelparenti.org>), to mention only a few of the many resources on this topic.

38. "World Scientists' Warning to Humanity" (as per note 19), p. 1.

39. For other examples of increasing holistic awareness see *Earth Island Journal* (pertaining to the environment) and the Web sites listed in appendix C. These resources will lead to many more.

40. R. Buckminster Fuller (with Kiyoshi Kuromiya, adjuvant), *Critical Path* (New York: St. Martin's, 1981), p. 251.

41. "Education for Comprehensivity" is the title of one of Fuller's essays. It appears in *Approaching the Benign Environment: The Franklin Lectures in the Sciences and Humanities,* ed. Taylor Littleton (University, Alabama: University of Alabama Press, 1970).

42. This sentence is paraphrased from Capra, *The Turning Point* (as per note 18), p. 38.

43. *Random House Webster's Unabridged Dictionary,* 2d ed.

44. Ron Miller, "Holistic Education in the United States: A 'New Paradigm' or a Cultural Struggle?" *Holistic Education Review* 6 (Dec. 1993): 12.

45. Buckminster Fuller in collaboration with E. J. Applewhite, *Synergetics: Explorations in the Geometry of Thinking* (New York: Macmillan, 1975), p. 3. Refer also to the section on synergy, this volume, chapter 2.

46. Ibid.; this example is adapted from pp. 6 and 7.

47. Ibid., pp. 6 and 7.

48. Much has been written about this issue. For examples, see the books listed in the first section of appendix B. See also Fritjof Capra, *The Turning Point* (as per note 18; also listed in appendix B), chapter 8 ("The Dark Side of Growth").

49. Fuller and Applewhite, *Synergetics* (as per note 45), p. 9.

50. *R. Buckminster Fuller on Education,* ed. Peter H. Wagschal and Robert D. Kahn (Amherst: University of Massachusetts Press, 1979), p. 11.

51. Many such resources are available, including those specifically for children. Appendixes B and C provide a starting point.

52. Two sources of information regarding the unseen realms are Rupert Sheldrake, *Seven Experiments That Could Change the World: A Do-It-Yourself Guide to Revolutionary Science* (New York: Riverhead Books, 1995); and Larry Dossey, M.D., *Reinventing Medicine: Beyond Mind-Body to a New Era of Healing* (Harper SanFrancisco, 1999).

53. Katya Walter, *Tao of Chaos: Merging East and West* (Austin, Texas: Kairos Center, 1994), pp. 22-23.

54. See *Random House Webster's Unabridged Dictionary,* 2d ed., s.v. "paradigm," second definition.

55. See Thomas S. Kuhn, *The Structure of Scientific Revolutions,* 2d ed. (1962; rpt. University of Chicago Press, 1970). (This book is listed in appendix B under Paradigm Shift/Science/Agriculture.)

56. Ibid., p. 208. See also p. 121 and chapter 13.

57. The information in this paragraph is paraphrased from Capra, *The Turning Point* (as per note 18), p. 47.

58. Also relevant in this context and an extension of it is the following, by the historian of cultures Thomas Berry:

> [A] total barrier between the human and the non-human . . . did not begin with the modern centuries. The support for what has happened existed within that part of our tradition that did not emerge from René Descartes or from Francis Bacon or from Isaac Newton.
>
> The barrier between the Western mode of consciousness and the natural world, and the consequent ethical deficiency in Western conscience, began in some manner with the biblical emphasis on the perception of the divine in historical events rather than within cosmological manifestation. . . . When in modern centuries the scientists gave us a natural world that came into being by purely random processes and without any spiritual meaning then the alienation of the human from the natural world was complete.

Thomas Berry, "Ethics and Ecology: A Paper Delivered to the Harvard Seminar on Environmental Values, Harvard University, 9 April 1996," *Environmental Ethics & Public Policy Program,* 5 April 2000 <www.hds.harvard.edu/ee/eth&ecol.htm>. See also Elisabet Sahtouris, *Gaia: The Human Journey from Chaos to Cosmos* (New York: Pocket Books, 1989), chapters 13-14.

59. See Capra, *The Turning Point* (as per note 18), pp. 60-61. See also David Bohm, *Wholeness and the Implicate Order* (London: Routledge & Kegan Paul, 1980), pp. 113 and 125. In this context essential reading is Thomas Berry, *The Great Work: Our Way into the Future* (New York: Bell Tower, 1999).

60. Capra, *The Turning Point,* p. 47.

61. For a detailed explanation of this paradigm shift see Capra, *The Turning Point.* The concepts presented are also the subject of *Mindwalk* (1991), a feature-length movie by Bernt Capra staring Liv Ullman, Sam Waterston, John Heard, and Ione Skye (available from Critics' Choice Video, P.O. Box 749, Itasca, Illinois 60143-0749 <www.criticschoicevideo.com>).

62. To learn more about new physics, see Fritjof Capra, *The Tao of Physics: An Exploration of the Parallels between Modern Physics and Eastern Mysticism,* 3d ed. (1975; rpt. Boston: Shambhala, 1991); and *The Turning Point.* See also David Bohm, *Wholeness and the Implicate Order* (as per note 59); Gary Zukav, *The Dancing Wu Li Masters: An Overview of the New Physics* (1979; rpt. New York: Bantam, 1980); and Fred Alan Wolf, *Taking the Quantum Leap: The New Physics for Nonscientists* (San Francisco: Harper & Row, 1981), to name a few of the many references available.

63. See Capra, *The Turning Point,* chapter 9 ("The Systems View of Life") and Bohm (as per note 59), p. 32.

64. Capra, *The Turning Point,* p. 48.

65. Ibid., p. 49.

66. Ibid., p. 265.

67. Some key references are listed in note 62. See also works by Buckminster Fuller and the molecular biologist Rupert Sheldrake, as well as Henri Bortoft, *The Wholeness of Nature: Goethe's Way toward a Science of Conscious Participation in Nature* (Hudson, New York: Lindisfarne Press, 1996). Other references are listed in appendix B under Paradigm Shift/Science/Agriculture.

68. Robert O. Becker, M.D., and Gary Selden, *The Body Electric: Electromagnetism and the Foundation of Life* (New York: William Morrow & Co., 1985), p. 230.

69. See Capra, *The Turning Point,* pp. 38-39, for these and other associations he draws.

70. Paraphrased from Douglas R. Hofstadter, *Gödel, Escher, Bach: An Eternal Golden Braid* (New York: Basic Books, 1979), p. 312. See also *The Encyclopedia of Eastern Philosophy and Religion* (as per note 31), p. 231.

71. Renée Weber, "The Tao of Physics Revisited: A Conversation with Fritjof Capra," *The Holographic Paradigm and Other Paradoxes: Exploring the Leading Edge of Science,* ed. Ken Wilber (Boulder: Shambhala Publications, 1982), p. 238. *Māyā,* which is from the Sanskrit, also has wider meanings than those noted in the text (see *The Encyclopedia of Eastern Philosophy and Religion* [as per note 31], p. 223).

72. Weber, "The Tao of Physics Revisited" (as per note 71), p. 243.
73. See Janine M. Benyus, *Biomimicry: Innovation Inspired by Nature* (New York: William Morrow & Co., 1997), chapter 7, "How Will We Conduct Business?"
74. Those who wish to investigate practical, holistically oriented approaches to community and economics may be interested in reading about the Sarvodaya Shramadana Movement (which translates as "the awakening of all through the sharing of labor or energy") in Sri Lanka; the Ghandian, Chipko, and other movements in India; and similar movements elsewhere. See also Frances Moore Lappé and Paul Martin Du Bois, *The Quickening of America: Rebuilding Our Nation, Remaking Our Lives* (San Francisco: Jossey-Bass Publishers, 1994), and books by Hazel Henderson (see appendix B). Holistic resources concerning each item on the list can be located through libraries and the World Wide Web (see also appendix B).
75. For an overview, see William Thomas, *Scorched Earth: The Military's Assault on the Environment* (Philadelphia: New Society Publishers, 1995), chapters 15 and 16. Given our current predicament, an environmental restoration corps needs to be created.
76. For example, in 1997 in the U.S., only 41.7 percent of the potentially recyclable paper and paperboard was recovered (see U.S. Environmental Protection Agency, Municipal and Industrial Solid Waste Division, Office of Solid Waste, *Characterization of Municipal Solid Waste in the United States: 1998 Update*, by Franklin Associates, a service of McLaren/Hart, Prairie Village, Kansas, July 1999, 12 July 2000 <www.epa.gov/epaoswer/non-hw/muncpl/msw98.htm> p. 30).
77. See "Happy Earth Day! We're Tree-Free!" *Earth Island Journal* 9 (Spring 1994): 19 (figures updated by Tom Rymsza, a kenaf expert and pioneer, and president of KP Products, Inc., Albuquerque, NM <www.visionpaper.com>, in a conversation on 17 July 2000). For further information, see the Web site for ReThink Paper, a project of the Earth Island Institute <www.rethinkpaper.org>; *Fiber Futures: Promoting Innovative Tree-Free and Recycled Fibers,* 16 June 2000 <www.fiberfutures. org>; "*Journal* Pioneers Tree-Free Paper," *Earth Island Journal* 8 (Summer 1993): 19; "Tree Free by 2003? Entrepreneurs are Hot on the Kenaf Paper Trail," *E: The Environmental Magazine* 4 (Nov./Dec. 1993): 22; and "Tree-Free Publishing," *Earth Island Journal* 11 (Summer 1996): 15.
78. Conversation with Tom Rymsza (see note 77), 16 July 2000.
79. See David Lorenz and David C. Pettijohn, *A New Industry Emerges: Making Construction Materials from Cellulosic Wastes* (Minneapolis: Institute for Local Self-Reliance, 1995), p. 2. (The Institute is listed in appendix C.) This figure does not include the amounts of straw (a major source of cellulose) that must be left on the ground for soil fertility. Marie Walsh, Ph.D., leader for the Resources Economics Task for the Bioenergy Feedstock Development Program at Oak Ridge National Laboratory, Oak Ridge, Tennessee, confirmed that the 160 million tons figure is "not unreasonable," noting that the quantity available is a function of price (26 June 2000 conversation with the author). The figure may be conservative, as other estimates have been considerably higher. (Accurate figures are difficult to come by; for example, there are widely varying opinions about what percent of wheat straw should be left in the field.)
80. Lorenz and Pettijohn (as per note 79), p. 1.
81. For example, see *The Millennium Whole Earth Catalog: Access to Tools and Ideas for the Twenty-first Century,* ed. Howard Rheingold (HarperSanFrancisco, 1994), a large, well-organized book of holistic strategies, products, and resources. According to Stewart Brand, creator of the *Whole Earth Catalog,* the insights of Buckminster Fuller initiated the catalog in 1967 (p. 36).
82. See especially works by Buckminster Fuller (shelter and design), John Robbins (food, health), Frances Moore Lappé et al. (food, economics, community building), and Hazel Henderson (economics). See also *The Millennium Whole Earth Catalog* (as per note 81) and *Earth Island Journal.* Another excellent resource is Jade Mountain, Inc.; see <www.jademountain.com>.

83. These definitions are adapted from *Random House Webster's Unabridged Dictionary,* 2d ed.
84. J. Krishnamurti, *Education and the Significance of Life* (1953; rpt. Harper-SanFrancisco, 1981), p. 11.

Chapter 2

Epigraph: Buckminster Fuller (with Kiyoshi Kuromiya, adjuvant) *Cosmography: A Posthumous Scenario for the Future of Humanity* (New York: Macmillan, 1992), p. 39. Fuller often omitted "the" and capitalized the first letter when referring to the universe. He wrote:

> Einstein operationally observed the Universe as a complex aggregate of non-simultaneously occurring, variously directioned, variously interwoven and overlapped, variously enduring events. I gave the name *scenario Universe* to Einstein's concept of Universe to distinguish it from a conventional single-frame picture, the concept of Universe favored by Newton. (p. 38)

Fuller defined "scenario" as "an aggregate of overlappingly introduced episodes, characters, themes, and only locally included births, lives, deaths, and other events" (p. 105). See also pp. 40-41, 64, 72-73, 105-6, and 236.

1. Bruce Wetterau, *The Presidential Medal of Freedom: Winners and Their Achievements* (Washington, D.C., Congressional Quarterly Inc., 1996), p. 319. Fuller received the award in 1983, a few months before he died. This medal, which was presented by President Reagan, is the highest civilian award in the U.S.
2. The first quotation is attributed to Marshall McLuhan (1911-1980), Canadian cultural historian and mass-communications theorist, although the former Fuller archivist Bonnie DeVarco notes that David Cort used the expression in an unpublished article in 1942. The second quotation appears in Fuller, *Critical Path* (as per chapter 1 note 40), book jacket.
3. *The Encyclopedia of the Environment,* The René Dubos Center for Human Environments, ed. Ruth A. Eblen and William R. Eblen (New York: Houghton Mifflin Co., 1994), p. 285.
4. Fuller, *Critical Path* (as per chapter 1 note 40), p. 125.
5. See chapter 1 note 41.
6. Fuller, *Cosmography* (as per chapter 2 epigraph note), p. 1.
7. *R. Buckminster Fuller on Education* (as per chapter 1 note 50), p. 77.
8. Fuller, *Critical Path* (as per chapter 1 note 40), p. 215. He wrote,

> If, for instance, we inbreed—by mating two fast-running horses—there is the mathematical probability of concentrating the fast-running genes but also of breeding in this special capability only by inadvertently breeding out the general adaptability to cope with the infrequent high-energy-concentrating events. For example, exquisitely designed birds' wings are a hindrance in walking, and the long bills of wading birds, which are perfect for marshland foraging, are relatively useless in other less specialized feeding.

9. Adapted from James Moffett, *The Universal Schoolhouse: Spiritual Awakening through Education* (San Francisco: Jossey-Bass, 1994), p. 96.
10. *R. Buckminster Fuller on Education* (as per chapter 1 note 50), p. 11.
11. *Your Private Sky: R. Buckminster Fuller, The Art of Design Science,* ed. Joachim Krausse and Claude Lichtenstein (Baden, Switzerland: Lars Müller Publishers, 1999), p. 12.
12. E. J. Applewhite, *Cosmic Fishing: An Account of Writing* Synergetics *with Buckminster Fuller* (New York: Macmillan, 1977), p. 65.
13. Fuller, *Operating Manual for Spaceship Earth* (as per chapter 1 epigraph note), p. 59.
14. *R. Buckminster Fuller on Education* (as per chapter 1 note 50), p. 39.
15. Paraphrased from *Buckminster Fuller Institute,* 2000, "Humanity's Option For Success," 2 May 2000 <www.bfi.org/option.htm>.

16. In addition to works by Fuller, another source of information about nature's methodology is Benyus (as per chapter 1 note 73).
17. Fuller, *Critical Path* (as per chapter 1 note 40), p. 126.
18. Fuller, *Operating Manual for Spaceship Earth* (as per chapter 1 epigraph note), p. 133.
19. Ibid.; see also *The Dymaxion Laboratory: What the Individual Can Do, Module I: The Big Picture, Course Materials* (Los Angeles: Buckminster Fuller Institute, 1991), p. 9-1.
20. See Fuller, *Operating Manual for Spaceship Earth* (as per chapter 1 epigraph note), p. 133. The following passages by Albert Einstein (1879-1955) offer insight into the theme of an intelligent universe:

> I cannot imagine a God who rewards and punishes the objects of his creation, whose purposes are modeled after our own—a God, in short, who is but a reflection of human frailty. . . . It is enough for me to contemplate the mystery of conscious life perpetuating itself through all eternity, to reflect upon the marvelous structure of the universe which we can dimly perceive and to try humbly to comprehend even an infinitesimal part of the intelligence manifested in Nature. . . .

> The scientist is possessed by the sense of universal causation. . . . His religious feeling takes the form of a rapturous amazement at the harmony of natural law, which reveals an intelligence of such superiority that, compared with it, all the systematic thinking and acting of human beings is an utterly insignificant reflection. . . . It is beyond question closely akin to that which has possessed the religious geniuses of all ages. . . .

> My religion consists of a humble admiration of the illimitable superior spirit who reveals himself in the slight details we are able to perceive with our frail and feeble minds. That deeply emotional conviction of the presence of a superior reasoning power, which is revealed in the incomprehensible universe, forms my idea of God.

Quoted in *The Quotable Einstein,* ed. Alice Calaprice (Princeton, New Jersey: Princeton University Press, 1996), pp. 150, 151, and 161.
21. Fuller and Applewhite, *Synergetics* (as per chapter 1 note 45), p. 3.
22. Fuller, *Cosmography* (as per chapter 2 epigraph note), p. 39.
23. Fuller and Applewhite, *Synergetics,* p. 4.
24. Fuller, Agel, and Fiore (as per chapter 1 epigraph note), p. 73A.
25. See ibid.
26. R. Buckminster Fuller, *Nine Chains to the Moon* (1938; rpt. Garden City, New York: Anchor Books/Doubleday, 1971), p. 259.
27. Fuller, Agel, and Fiore, p. 34A.
28. See Fuller, "Education for Comprehensivity" (as per chapter 1 note 41), p. 67.
29. See R. Buckminster Fuller, *50 Years of the Design Science Revolution and the World Game* (Philadelphia: World Resources Inventory, 1969), pp. 106-7; and J. Baldwin, *BuckyWorks: Buckminster Fuller's Ideas for Today* (New York: John Wiley & Sons, 1996), p. 189. Baldwin notes, for example,

> The transparent, climate-controlling weather shields would . . . relieve New York's notorious, stifling summer heat. In winter, solar gain and wind deflection would produce balmy weather inside the buildings and in the streets, substantially reducing the need to individually heat inefficient buildings. Bucky calculated the dome's total skin surface would be less than 5 percent of the total wall and roof area of the buildings it covered, giving immense thermal advantage.
>   The project is technically and economically feasible; geodesic domes get stronger as they get bigger; and domes of this size would get additional pneumatic support from the air inside. . . . Much of the slim structural network would be too far above the street to be visible. Bucky calculated that saved

> energy and the elimination of expensive snow removal would quickly pay for the
> domes. . . .
> The drastic proposal may be extreme, but it does get you thinking. That's
> just what Bucky had in mind.

30. For illustrated examples see Fuller and Applewhite, *Synergetics,* p. 25. See also
Donald E. Ingber, "The Architecture of Life," *Scientific American* 278 (Jan. 1998):
48-57; and *Your Private Sky* (as per note 11), pp. 444-51.

31. For one example see "Nanotubes for Flat Panel Displays," *Trimtab: Bulletin of the
Buckminster Fuller Institute* 12 (Summer 1999): 6. See also Amy C. Edmondson, *A
Fuller Explanation: The Synergetic Geometry of R. Buckminster Fuller* (Boston: Birk-
hauser Boston, 1987), pp. xix-xx.

32. "Malthusian" refers to the theories of English economist and clergyman Thomas
R. Malthus (1766-1834), which state that "population tends to increase faster, at
a geometrical ratio, than the means of subsistence, which increases at an arith-
metical ratio, and that this will result in an inadequate supply of the goods
supporting life unless war, famine, or disease reduces the population or the
increase of population is checked" (from *Random House Webster's Unabridged
Dictionary,* 2d ed.). See also Fuller, *Critical Path* (as per chapter 1 note 40).

33. Fuller, *Critical Path,* p. 133.

34. Baldwin (as per note 29), p. 15.

35. Edmondson (as per note 31), p. 284.

36. R. Buckminster Fuller, *Intuition,* 2d ed. (1972; rpt. San Luis Obispo, California:
Impact Publishers, 1983), p. 41.

37. R. Buckminster Fuller, *Tetrascroll: Goldilocks and the Three Bears, A Cosmic Fairy
Tale* (New York: St. Martin's Press, 1975), p. 30.

38. Fuller, *Critical Path,* pp. 141-42.

39. Ibid., p. 142.

40. Fuller, *Intuition* (as per note 36), p. 96.

41. Fuller, *Critical Path,* p. 142.

42. Ibid., p. 143.

43. Fuller, *Intuition,* p. 96.

44. Fuller, *Tetrascroll,* p. 30.

45. Fuller, *Critical Path,* p. 246.

46. Ibid., p. 143.

47. See ibid., pp. 141-46, for an elegant presentation of precession and how realizing
its existence and interworkings affected Fuller's life. See also *Intuition* (as per note
36), pp. 41-50 and 96.

48. Fuller, *Intuition,* pp. 41-42.

49. Fuller, *Cosmography* (as per chapter 2 epigraph note), p. 51.

50. This concise definition is from Ehrlich and Ehrlich (as per chapter 1 note 14),
p. 139.

51. Fuller, *Critical Path,* p. 275. For further insight see Stuart Kauffman, *At Home in
the Universe: The Search for the Laws of Self-Organization and Complexity* (New York:
Oxford University Press), pp. 9-10; and Louise B. Young, *The Unfinished Universe*
(New York: Simon and Schuster, 1986), chapter 6, "Entropy and Evolution."

52. Fuller, *Critical Path,* p. 276.

53. Ibid., pp. 27-28.

54. Fuller has much to say about regeneration in *Critical Path.*

55. Fuller, *Cosmography* (as per chapter 2 epigraph note), p. 261. See also note 19.

56. Fuller and Applewhite, *Synergetics* (as per chapter 1 note 45), p. 13.

57. Fuller, *Critical Path,* p. 164. See note 59 for the origin of the word "Dymaxion."

58. Ibid., p. 136; "*Life* Presents R. Buckminster Fuller's Dymaxion World," *Life* 14
(1 March 1943): 41-55.

59. "The Dymaxion American," *Time* (10 Jan. 1964): 48. Edmondson (as per note 31)
states in the glossary of her book: "Dymaxion: Fuller's trademark word, created by
Marshall Fields Department Store in the late 1920s, for use in promotion of

exhibit featuring Fuller's revolutionary house design" (p. 282). See also Fuller, *Critical Path* (as per chapter 1 note 40).

60. Lewis Thomas, *The Lives of a Cell: Notes of a Biology Watcher* (1974; rpt. New York: Bantam Books, 1975), p. 4.
61. Fuller, *Critical Path,* p. 172.
62. Ibid.
63. R. Buckminster Fuller, "Architecture Out of the Laboratory," *Student Publication* (University of Michigan College of Architecture and Design), vol. 1 (Spring 1955): 27.
64. *R. Buckminster Fuller on Education* (as per chapter 1 note 50), p. 52.
65. Fuller, *Critical Path,* p. 173.
66. Ibid., p. 169.
67. Ibid., p. 181.
68. Ibid., p. 169.
69. Ibid., p. 174.
70. Ibid.
71. Ibid., pp. 175 and 179.
72. Ibid., p. 183.
73. Ibid.
74. Ibid., pp. 173-74.
75. See ibid., pp. 174 and 175. Fuller wrote:

> The proposed U.N. East River Blackwell's ledge installation of the 200-foot Geoscope was brought to the attention of U Thant when he was the Secretary General of the United Nations. It appealed to him so much that he gave a luncheon at New York City's Hotel Pierre for me and all the ambassadors to the U.N. from around the Earth. It was well attended, with more than half of the world's permanent ambassadors to the U.N. present. He had me give a thorough presentation speech describing the 200-footer. It met with great favor. Thereafter, on a number of prominent occasions, U Thant represented the concept. The estimated cost at that time was $10 million. Inflation would make it about $50 million today [in 1981, when *Critical Path* was published]. There was no visible source of funding. The U.N. itself did not have any funds for such a purpose. The development of the popularity of World Game and the increasing need for the 200-foot Geoscope might suggest that its realization may not be far off. (pp. 183-84)

See also Fuller, Agel, and Fiore (as per chapter 1 epigraph note), p. 172B.
76. Baldwin (as per note 29), pp. 197 and 199.
77. Some of Fuller's ideas on the subject of world governance appear in *R. Buckminster Fuller on Education* (as per chapter 1 note 50), pp. 159 and 45-46; and in *Critical Path* (as per chapter 1 note 40), pp. 341-42.
78. Baldwin (as per note 29), p. 199.
79. Fuller, *Critical Path,* p. 184.
80. Baldwin (as per note 29), p. 199. This 1996 book states the number of entries for every country as 1,000; as of 1999, the figure was 2,000 (Feb. 1999 communication to the author from Medard Gabel, executive director, World Game Institute).
81. Fuller, *Intuition* (as per note 36), p. 40.
82. Fuller, "Education for Comprehensivity" (as per chapter 1 note 41), p. 63.
83. Ibid., p. 65.
84. Ibid.
85. R. Buckminster Fuller, *Grunch of Giants* (New York: St. Martin's Press, 1983), p. 33.
86. Fuller, *50 Years of the Design Science Revolution and the World Game* (as per note 29), p. 116.
87. Fuller, "Education for Comprehensivity," p. 50.
88. Ibid., p. 51.
89. Ibid.

90. Ibid., p. 46.
91. Fuller, *Critical Path,* p. xxxiv.
92. Ibid., p. xvii.
93. Fuller, *Intuition* (as per note 36), p. 138.
94. Fuller, "Education for Comprehensivity," p. 66.
95. Fuller, *Critical Path,* p. 203.
96. *R. Buckminster Fuller on Education* (as per chapter 1 note 50), p. 153.
97. R. Buckminster Fuller, interview by Steve Edwards, *2 On The Town,* KCBS-TV, Los Angeles, 25 June 1982 (rebroadcast 1 Aug. 1983).
98. Richard J. Brenneman, *Fuller's Earth: A Day with Bucky and the Kids* (New York: St. Martin's Press, 1984) p. 109.
99. *R. Buckminster Fuller on Education,* pp. 37-38.
100. Fuller, "Education for Comprehensivity," p. 68.
101. Ibid., p. 69.
102. R. Buckminster Fuller, "Integrity: Humans Are Now in a Final Exam, and the Questions May Not Be What You Thought They Were," *The Review* (Nov./ Dec. 1982): 5.
103. Fuller, *Critical Path,* p. 199.
104. Ibid., pp. 198-99.
105. Fuller, *Cosmography* (as per chapter 2 epigraph note), p. 7.
106. See Fuller, *50 Years of the Design Science Revolution and the World Game* (as per note 29), p. 96. See also Baldwin (as per note 29), pp. 186-87.
107. Adapted from Baldwin, pp. 94 and 96; see also pp. 88-103.
108. Fuller, *Cosmography,* p. 7.
109. Applewhite (as per note 12), p. 74.
110. Edmondson (as per note 31), p. xx.
111. Ibid., p. 283. See also Fuller and Applewhite, *Synergetics* (as per chapter 1 note 45) and Buckminster Fuller in collaboration with E. J. Applewhite, *Synergetics 2: Further Explorations in the Geometry of Thinking* (New York: Macmillan, 1979).
112. Fuller and Applewhite, *Synergetics,* p. 26.
113. John McHale, *R. Buckminster Fuller* (New York: George Braziller, 1962), pp. 113 and 115. This quotation by Fuller is "from a letter in answer to an inquiry by Collier's Reference Service regarding Fuller's geometry, October 1959" (p. 113). See pp. 113-15 for axioms; see also Fuller and Applewhite, *Synergetics,* pp. 63-67.
114. "Escape from the Dark Ages," Robert Anton Wilson, *Trajectories* 1 (Spring 1993): 4. This article is a review of Fuller's *Cosmography.*
115. Edmondson (as per note 31), pp. xix-xx.
116. Adapted from Baldwin (as per note 29), p. 199.
117. See Fuller, *Critical Path* (as per chapter 1 note 40), p. 55.
118. Fuller, Agel, and Fiore (as per chapter 1 epigraph note), p. 179A.
119. Brenneman (as per note 98), p. 103.
120. R. Buckminster Fuller, *Earth, Inc.* (Garden City, New York: Anchor Press/ Doubleday, 1973), p. 127.
121. Fuller, "Education for Comprehensivity," p. 53.
122. Fuller, Agel, and Fiore (as per chapter 1 epigraph note), p. 154B.
123. See Brenneman (as per note 98), pp. 30-31.
124. Fuller, Agel, and Fiore, p. 120A.
125. See Brenneman, p. 41.
126. Fuller, *Critical Path,* p. 55.
127. *R. Buckminster Fuller on Education* (as per chapter 1 note 50), p. 130.
128. Fuller, *Cosmography,* pp. 34-35. See pp. 33-39 for all twelve discoveries.
129. Fuller, Agel, and Fiore (as per chapter 1 epigraph note), pp. 94B-99B.
130. R. Buckminster Fuller and Cam Smith, *Buckminster Fuller to Children of Earth* (Garden City, New York: Doubleday, 1972), n.p.
131. Derived from Gerhard Hirschfeld, *An Essay on Mankind* (New York: Philosophical Library, 1957), p. 75.
132. Fuller and Applewhite, *Synergetics 2* (as per note 111), p. 50.

133. Fuller, *Earth, Inc.* (as per note 120), pp. 10-11.
134. Fuller and Applewhite, *Synergetics* (as per chapter 1 note 45), p. 13.
135. Buckminster Fuller had much more to say about education than can be presented in this overview. See "Education for Comprehensivity" (as per chapter 1 note 41), *R. Buckminster Fuller on Education* (as per chapter 1 note 50), *Critical Path* (as per chapter 1 note 40), and other works by Fuller. His views on education are consolidated in *The Educational Philosophy of R. Buckminster Fuller,* a 1985 dissertation by Alex Gerber Jr. (available from Micrographics Department, Doheny Library, University of Southern California, Los Angeles, CA 90089-0182, or through the Interlibrary Loan System).
136. *R. Buckminster Fuller on Education* (as per chapter 1 note 50), p. 51.
137. Fuller, *50 Years of the Design Science Revolution and the World Game* (as per note 29), p. 27. Fuller's "Conning Tower" concept was first published in *Shelter* magazine in 1932. He wrote about the same concept even earlier, in an unpublished 1928 manuscript entitled "Lightful Houses" (Fuller Archives).
138. *R. Buckminster Fuller on Education* (as per chapter 1 note 50), pp. 42-43.
139. For example, see Fritjof Capra, *The Web of Life: A New Scientific Understanding of Living Systems* (New York: Anchor Books/Doubleday, 1996), pp. 69 and 70. Capra observes,

> Today . . . computers and the many other "information technologies" . . . are rapidly becoming autonomous and totalitarian, redefining our basic concepts and eliminating alternative worldviews. . . . [T]his is typical of the "megatechnologies" that have come to dominate industrial societies around the world. Increasingly, all forms of culture are being subordinated to technology, and technological innovation, rather than the increase in human well-being, has become synonymous with progress. (pp. 69-70)

> The use of computers in schools is based on the now outdated view of human beings as information processors, which continually reinforces erroneous mechanistic concepts of thinking, knowledge, and communication. Information is presented as the basis of thinking, whereas in reality the human mind thinks with ideas, not with information. (p. 70)

140. See Edmondson (as per note 31), chapter 1.
141. Contact the Buckminster Fuller Institute for information about modeling kits (see appendix C).
142. Calvin Tomkins, "Profiles: In the Outlaw Area," *The New Yorker* (8 Jan. 1966): 52.
143. For a more detailed analysis of Buckminster Fuller's education philosophy vis-à-vis that of Montessori, see Gerber (as per note 135).
144. R. Buckminster Fuller, *4D Timelock* (1928; rpt. Corrales, New Mexico: The Lama Foundation, 1972), p. 18.
145. E. M. Standing, *The Montessori Revolution in Education* (1962; rpt. New York: Schocken Books, 1966), p. 85 (originally published as *The Montessori Method: A Revolution in Education* [Fresno, California: The Academy Library Guild, 1962]).
146. Fuller's essay "Mistake Mystique" was originally published in *East West Journal* (April 1977). It also appears in *R. Buckminster Fuller on Education* (as per chapter 1 note 50) and in the 1983 edition of *Intuition* (as per note 36).
147. Fuller, *Intuition* (as per note 36), p. 95.
148. Fuller, *Intuition,* p. 91.
149. Ibid.
150. Paraphrased from *Integrity Day: A Meeting with Buckminster Fuller, February 26, 1983* (Los Angeles: Buckminster Fuller Institute, 1983), p. 2.
151. Fuller, *Intuition,* p. 94.
152. R. Buckminster Fuller and Anwar Dil, *Humans in Universe* (New York: Mouton, 1983), p. 130.
153. Fuller, *Cosmography* (as per chapter 2 epigraph note), p. 263.
154. Ibid., p. 248.
155. Fuller, *Operating Manual for Spaceship Earth* (as per chapter 1 epigraph note), p. 49.

156. Applewhite (as per note 12), p. 7.
157. For more information on this topic see Benyus (as per chapter 1 note 73).
158. A more detailed analysis of criticisms pertaining to Buckminster Fuller's philosophy appears in Gerber (as per note 135). See also "The Skeptic," a chapter in Hugh Kenner, *A Guided Tour of Buckminster Fuller* (New York: William Morrow & Co., 1973).
159. Fuller and Dil (as per note 152), p. 43.
160. See "The Dymaxion American" (as per note 59).
161. Baldwin (as per note 29), p. 232.
162. These books are referenced in chapter 2 note 31, chapter 1 note 45, and chapter 2 note 111.
163. As per note 98.
164. *The Buckminster Fuller Institute* brochure (Sebastopol, California: Buckminster Fuller Institute, 2000). See also the Buckminster Fuller Institute's Web site listed in appendix C.
165. *The Buckminster Fuller Institute* brochure (as per note 164).
166. See "Fuller Archive Finds New Home at Stanford University," *Trimtab: Bulletin of the Buckminster Fuller Institute* 12 (Summer 1999): 1 and 5; see also James Sterngold, "The Face of the Future Is a Thing of the Past," *New York Times,* 17 July 1999.
167. William Marlin, "Buckminster Fuller: 'A Terrific Bundle of Experience,'" *Christian Science Monitor,* 23 Sept. 1983, p. 13.
168. Applewhite, p. 57. T. S. Eliot once held the Charles Eliot Norton Chair of poetry (see Kenner [as per note 158], p. 79).
169. Kenner, pp. 11, 300, and 314.
170. "Peter Wagschal on the 'Future of Education,'" *Trimtab: Bulletin of the Buckminster Fuller Institute* 7 (Spring 1993): 6.
171. Fuller, *Earth, Inc.,* p. 101.
172. Fuller, *Critical Path* (as per chapter 1 note 36), p. 266.
173. *R. Buckminster Fuller on Education* (as per chapter 1 note 45), p. 53.

Chapter 3

Epigraph: Thomas Merton, *The Way of Chuang Tzu* (New York: New Directions, 1969), p. 40.

1. *The Encyclopedia of Eastern Philosophy and Religion* (as per chapter 1 note 31), p. 356. See also note 4 (below).
2. Merton (as per chapter 3 epigraph note), p. 15.
3. John Blofeld, *Taoism: The Road to Immortality* (Boulder: Shambhala Publications, 1978), pp. 90-93. Blofeld (1913-1987) was a British author, translator, and scholar of Taoism.
4. Scholarly opinions vary regarding the biographical details of Lao-tzu's life and the origins of the *Tao Te Ching,* a work generally attributed to him. According to the introduction to *Tao Te Ching,* trans. Man-Ho Kwok, Martin Palmer, and Jay Ramsay (Rockport, Mass.: Element Inc., 1993):

> There is some doubt as to whether Lao Tzu himself ever existed. Supposed to have been written in one night, the *Tao Te Ching* in fact encompasses texts which probably cover a time span of eight hundred years. Seen as the classic of Taoism, it was in use long before Taoism was an identified school. . . .
>
> The traditional story of the *Tao Te Ching's* origin is contained in a biography of Lao Tzu and was first written down at the start of the first century BC by the great historian of China, Ssu-ma Ch'ien. This means it was committed to paper some four hundred years after Lao Tzu was thought to have lived. Ssu-ma Ch'ien found it very difficult to find any firm details about Lao Tzu—a fact which he acknowledges in his book. . . .
>
> Lao Tzu is not a proper name. It is an honorific title and simply means 'the Old Master'. Thus it is impossible to deduce anything from it about the original name of the person to whom it was applied. (p. 7)

5. See John Blofeld, *Taoist Mysteries and Magic* (1973; rpt. Boulder: Shambhala Publications, 1982), chapters 4 and 6. Books containing the philosophies of Lao-tzu and Chuang-tzu appear in appendix B.

6. Merton (as per chapter 3 epigraph note), p. 152.

7. See *The Zen Teaching of Huang Po: On the Transmission of Mind,* trans. John Blofeld (New York: Grove Press, 1958), pp. 18-19 and 29-34. Blofeld notes, "The text indicates that Huang Po [a ninth-century Zen master] was not entirely satisfied with his choice of the word 'Mind' to symbolize the inexpressible Reality beyond the reach of conceptual thought, for he more than once explains that the One Mind is not really mind at all. But he had to use some term or other, and 'Mind' had often been used by his predecessors" (p. 18). Furthermore, "Zen followers (who have much in common with mystics of other faiths) do not use the term 'God', being wary of its dualistic and anthropomorphic implications. They prefer to talk of 'the Absolute' or 'the One Mind', for which they employ many synonyms according to the aspect to be emphasized in relation to something finite. Thus, the word 'Buddha' is used as a synonym for the Absolute as well as in the sense of Gautama, the Enlightened One, for it is held that the two are identical" (p. 16). See also note 17.

8. Adapted from Miller (as per chapter 1 note 44), p. 12.

9. Moffett (as per chapter 2 note 9), p. 22.

10. Ibid., p. xix.

11. Aldous Huxley, *The Perennial Philosophy* (1944; rpt. New York: Harper & Row, 1970), pp. vii and viii.

12. See James Glanz, "Cosmic Motion Revealed," *Science* 282 (18 Dec. 1998): 2156-57. See also Floyd E. Bloom, "Breakthroughs 1998," ibid., p. 2193. The announcement on the cover of this issue states, "The Accelerating Universe: Breakthrough of the Year."

13. For further insight into this theme see chapter 2 note 20. See also Peter Tompkins and Christopher Bird, *The Secret Life of Plants* (New York: Harper & Row, 1973) and *Secrets of the Soil* (New York: Harper & Row, 1989); Robert Augros and George Stanciu, *The New Biology: Discovering the Wisdom in Nature* (Boston: Shambhala, 1988); Sheldrake (as per chapter 1 note 52); Walter (as per chapter 1 note 53); Renée Weber, *Dialogues with Scientists and Sages: The Search for Unity* (New York: Routledge & Kegan Paul, 1986), pp. 100 and 235 (portions of Weber's interviews with David Bohm); and Fuller, *Critical Path* (as per chapter 1 note 40), pp. 27, 152-59, and 345-46. These books are also listed in appendix B.

14. Ivan Illich, *Celebration of Awareness* (1970; rpt. New York: Anchor Books/ Doubleday, 1971), p. 152.

15. Bohm (as per chapter 1 note 59), p. xi.

16. Quoted from Diogenes Laertius, *Lives of Eminent Philosophers,* 2.32, in John Bartlett, *Familiar Quotations: A Collection of Passages, Phrases and Proverbs Traced to Their Sources,* 14th ed. (1855; rpt. Boston: Little, Brown, 1968), p. 87.

17. *The Zen Teaching of Huang Po* (as per note 7), pp. 34 and 69. Huang Po explained, "To say that Mind [see note 7] is no-mind implies something existent. Let there be a silent understanding and no more. Away with all thinking and explaining. Then we may say that the Way of Words has been cut off and movements of the mind eliminated. This Mind is the pure Buddha-Source inherent in all men" (pp. 34-35). In a footnote the translator wrote, "In other words, Mind is an arbitrary term for something that cannot properly be expressed in words."

18. See Alan Watts with the collaboration of Al Chung-liang Huang, *Tao: The Watercourse Way* (New York: Pantheon Books, 1975); and Lao-tzu, *Tao Te Ching,* trans. Gia-fu Feng and Jane English (New York: Alfred A. Knopf, 1972), verse 8.

19. Abraham H. Maslow, *Religions, Values, and Peak Experiences* (1964; rpt. New York: Penguin Books, 1976), p. 83.

20. Ibid., p. 57.

21. These definitions are adapted and quoted from *Random House Webster's Unabridged Dictionary,* 2d ed.

22. "The Message of the Myth," exec. prods. Joan Conner and Alvin H. Perlmutter, exec. ed. Bill Moyers, program 2, *Joseph Campbell and The Power of Myth, with Bill Moyers* (audiotape), Apostrophe S Productions in association with Alvin H. Perlmutter, Inc. and Public Affairs Television, Inc., 1988. All six programs appear as a single reference in appendix B under Philosophy/Spirituality/Poetry.

23. Ibid.

24. Ibid.

25. Ibid.

26. Ibid. Bill Moyers, who was the interviewer, used these latter two terms in a question he posed to Campbell.

27. "Global village" is defined as "the world, especially as the home of all nations and peoples living interdependently [term introduced by the book *War and Peace in the Global Village* (1968) by Marshall McLuhan and Quentin Fiore]," *Random House Webster's Unabridged Dictionary,* 2d ed.

28. "The Message of the Myth" (as per note 22).

29. Ibid.

30. For example, see Barry Farrell, "*Playboy* Interview: R. Buckminster Fuller, a Candid Conversation with the Visionary Architect/Inventor/Philosopher," *Playboy* (Feb. 1972). Fuller said, "You find a thinker like Lao-tse; the record is clear illustrating the brilliant, incisive, economical thinking that has gone on there. [The people of ancient China and India] could see very clearly all the things I've been saying" (p. 200). See also Fuller, Agel, and Fiore (as per chapter 1 epigraph note), in which Fuller stated, "It is possible to concur with the 5,000-year-old philosophy of the Bhagavad-Gita, which says: 'Action is a product of the qualities inherent in nature'" (p. 96A). There have been widely differing estimates of when the *Bhagavad-Gītā* was composed (see *The Encyclopedia of Eastern Philosophy and Religion* [as per chapter 1 note 31], pp. 31 and 211). As to its origins, however, according to *Bhagavad-gītā As It Is* (trans. A. C. Bhaktivedanta Swami Prabhupāda [Los Angeles: The Bhaktivedanta Book Trust, 1983]):

    > Although widely published and read by itself, *Bhagavad-gītā* originally appears as an episode in the *Mahābhārata,* the epic Sanskrit history of the ancient world. The *Mahābhārata* tells of events leading up to the present Age of Kali. It was at the beginning of this age, some fifty centuries ago, that Lord Krsna spoke *Bhagavad-gītā* to His friend and devotee Arjuna. (p. xiii)

31. Baldwin (as per chapter 2 note 29), p. 15.

32. Fuller, *Intuition* (as per chapter 2 note 36), p. 61.

33. Fuller, *Critical Path* (as per chapter 1 note 40), p. 27. See also note 13.

34. Quoted in Robert Anton Wilson (as per chapter 2 note 114), p. 4.

35. Fuller, *Critical Path,* p. 152. See also note 13.

36. Lao-tzu (as per note 18), verse 1.

37. Brenneman (as per chapter 2 note 98), p. 23.

38. Fuller, *Critical Path,* p. 159.

39. A fascinating chart entitled "Underlying Order in Randomness" in Fuller's book *Operating Manual for Spaceship Earth* (as per chapter 1 epigraph note), pp. 68-69, illustrates this concept. See also Capra, *The Web of Life* (as per chapter 2 note 139), and Walter (as per chapter 1 note 53) for relevant information (both are listed in appendix B). See also Kauffman (as per chapter 2 note 51). Capra notes,

    > A new language for understanding the complex, highly integrative systems of life has . . . emerged. Different scientists call it by different names—"dynamical systems theory," "the theory of complexity," "nonlinear dynamics," "network dynamics," and so on. Chaotic attractors, fractals, dissipative structures, self-organization, and autopoietic networks are some of its key concepts. (p. xviii)

    It is noteworthy that Fuller's explorations in this area, based on the data of his synergetic geometry, were published as early as 1963.

40. Paraphrased from Moffett (as per chapter 2 note 9), pp. 43-44.

41. See Edward Goldsmith et al., *Imperiled Planet: Restoring Our Endangered Ecosystems* (Cambridge: MIT Press, 1990), p. 87. See chapter 1 note 26 for related references.
42. The evolutionary economist and futurist Hazel Henderson observes that "CSOs [are] sometimes still called Non-Government Organizations (NGOs)," but "re-definition of citizen organizations is now crucial, since the WTO [World Trade Organization] defines IBM, Microsoft, GM, and other global corporations as 'NGOs'" (Hazel Henderson for the New Economics Foundation in association with Focus on the Global South, *Beyond Globalization: Shaping a Sustainable Global Economy* [Kumarian Press, 1999], pp. 22 and 59).
43. See, for example, Mark Hertsgaard, *Earth Odyssey: Around the World in Search of Our Environmental Future* (New York: Broadway Books, 1998), chapter 9 ("Living in Hope"). See also Daniel Quinn, *Beyond Civilization: Humanity's Next Great Adventure* (New York: Harmony Books, 1999).
44. Thomas Berry, "The Seduction of WonderWorld," *Edges: New Planetary Patterns* 3 (June 1990): 13 and 14 (*Edges* magazine is published by the Canadian Instutute of Cultural Affairs, Toronto, Ontario, Canada). Berry's most recent book, *The Great Work: Our Way into the Future,* which discusses similar themes, is listed in appendix B.
45. Merton (as per chapter 3 epigraph note), pp. 136-37.
46. Lao-tzu (as per note 18), verse 9.
47. See *Ecology, Economics, Ethics: The Broken Circle,* ed. F. Herbert Bormann and Stephen R. Kellert (New Haven, Conn.: Yale University Press, 1991).
48. Rabindranath Tagore, *Fireflies* (1928; rpt. New York: The Macmillan Co., 1951), p. 92. Tagore was the Nobel Laureate for poetry in 1913.
49. This parable was referred to by the English journalist Malcom Muggeridge. See Henry Mitchell, "St. Mug Speaketh: A Mouthful on the Perils Of Seeking an Earthly Paradise," *Washington Post,* 25 Jan. 1978. There is no indication of the origination of the concept. The "boiled frog syndrome" is also referred to (among other places) in Robert Ornstein and Paul Ehrlich, *New World New Mind: Moving toward Conscious Evolution* (New York: Doubleday, 1989), pp. 74-75.
50. Lao-tzu (as per note 18), verse 40.
51. Sengtsan, *hsin hsin ming* [verses on the faith-mind], trans. Richard B. Clarke (Buffalo, New York: White Pine Press, 1984), n.p. This booklet is listed in appendix B under Philosophy/Spirituality/Poetry. The book *hsin hsin ming* also appears in Dennis Genpo Merzel, *The Eye Never Sleeps: Striking to the Heart of Zen,* ed. Stephen Muho Proskauer (Boston: Shambhala, 1991).
52. Lao-tzu, *Tao Te Ching,* a new English version, with foreword and notes, by Stephen Mitchell (New York: Harper & Row, 1988), verse 21.
53. Ibid., verse 11.
54. A brief explanation of the Standard Model appears in *The New Encyclopædia Britannica,* 15th ed., s.v. "standard model," which describes it as

> the combination of two theories of particle physics into a single framework to describe all interactions of subatomic particles, except those due to gravity. The two components of the standard model are electroweak theory, which describes interactions via the electromagnetic and weak forces, and quantum chromo-dynamics, the theory of the strong nuclear force. Both these theories are gauge field theories, which describe the interactions between particles in terms of the exchange of intermediary "messenger" particles that have one unit of intrinsic angular momentum, or spin.
>
> In addition to these force-carrying particles, the standard model encompasses two families of subatomic particles that build up matter and that have spins of one-half unit. These particles are the quarks and the leptons, and there are six varieties, or "flavours," of each, related in pairs in three "generations" of increasing mass. Everyday matter is built from the members of the lightest

generation: the protons and neutrons of atomic nuclei; the electron that orbits within atoms and participates in binding atoms together to make molecules and more complex structures; and the electron-neutrino that plays a role in radio-activity and so influences the stability of matter. . . .

55. Of course there may be other forces not yet discovered. See Sheldrake (as per chapter 1 note 52), p. 94. (This book is also listed in appendix B under Paradigm Shift/Science/Agriculture.) Sheldrake says that connections between pets and owners, between pigeons and their homes, and between the members of termite colonies are examples of possible fields (or a single field) to be discovered. He says:

> Sooner or later, any new kind of field must in some way be related to the known fields of physics, even if this relationship becomes clear only in the light of a unified field theory of the future. Such a unified theory would need to be far larger in scope than any attempted to date, since institutional physics has so far ignored the possibility of any fundamentally new field phenomena in the realm of life. (p. 96)

See also Dossey (as per chapter 1 note 52).
56. Lao-tzu (as per note 18), verse 42.
57. See Brian Greene, *The Elegant Universe: Superstrings, Hidden Dimensions, and the Quest for the Ultimate Theory* (New York: W. W. Norton & Co., 1999), p. 14.
58. Lao-tzu (as per note 52), verse 41.
59. *Crow with No Mouth, Ikkyū: 15th Century Zen Master,* versions by Stephen Berg (Port Townsend, Washington: Copper Canyon Press, 1989), p. 28.
60. *The Kabir Book: Forty-Four of the Ecstatic Poems of Kabir,* versions by Robert Bly (Boston: Beacon Press, 1977), pp. 4-5.
61. See Marcia Baringa, "Watching the Brain Remake Itself," *Science* 266 (2 Dec. 1994): 1475; Urmila Ranadive, "Phantom Limbs and Rewired Brains," *Technology Review* 100 (Jan. 1997): 17-18; and Joannie M. Schrof, "Stroke Busters: New Treatments in the Fight Against 'Brain Attacks,'" *U.S. News & World Report* 126 (15 March 1999): 64-65.
62. *The Encyclopedia of Eastern Philosophy and Religion* (as per chapter 1 note 31), p. 364.
63. Fuller, *Cosmography* (as per chapter 2 epigraph note), pp. 117-18.
64. See, for example, *Remineralize the Earth* (a magazine published since 1986 and available online at <www.remineralize-the-earth.org>) and related materials.

Epigraph

The Upanishads, trans. Alistair Shearer and Peter Russell (New York: Harper Clophon Books, 1978), p. 12. "The word 'upanishad' is derived from the Sanskrit root SHAD, meaning 'to sit,' 'to settle,' or 'to approach,' and from the prefixes UPA, meaning 'near,' and NI, meaning 'down.' An 'upanishad' is thus 'a sitting down near'" an enlightened teacher and settling one's mind in order to receive spiritual teaching (p. 11). Transmitted by ancient masters approximately 5,000 years ago, the Upanishads "form the final portion of the *shruti* (the revealed part of the Veda) and the principal basis of Vedanta, the philosophical conclusion derived from the Vedas. They are distinguished, valued highly by seekers of wisdom, for their tran-scendent breadth and powerful freedom of thought" (*The Encyclopedia of Eastern Philosophy and Religion* [as per chapter 1 note 31], p. 392). Some scholars believe the information in *The Upanishads* to be far older than 5,000 years.

Appendix A

1. Self-created courses on wholeness can be embarked upon individually or by groups of parents, teachers, students, professors, administrators, curriculum specialists, corporate and governmental educators, environmental educators, corporate boards, and other decision makers. Appendixes B and C will be helpful.
2. Publication information for these books is listed in appendix B.
3. There are approximately 700 existing interpretations of Lao-tzu's *Tao Te Ching* (according to Man-jan Cheng, *Lao-tzu: "My words are very easy to understand": Lectures on the Tao Teh Ching,* trans. Tam C. Gibbs [Richmond, California: North Atlantic Books, 1981], p. 1). One of them is noted in appendix B under Philosophy/Spirituality/Poetry.
4. See chapter 3 note 49.
5. See Fritjof Capra's chart in appendix E.
6. Fuller, *Critical Path* (as per chapter 1 note 40), p. 251.
7. See *Random House Webster's Unabridged Dictionary,* 2d ed., s.v. "integrity," second definition.
8. See chapter 3 note 11.
9. See *Ecology, Economics, Ethics: The Broken Circle* (as per chapter 3 note 47).
10. As per chapter 2 note 2.
11. Applewhite (as per chapter 2 note 12), p. 65.
12. As per chapter 1 note 41; see also page 49, this volume.
13. Publication information for these books is listed in appendix B.
14. "Grunch" is Fuller's acronym for "Gross Universal Cash Heist."
15. See appendix B for a longer (though not all-inclusive) listing of books by or about Fuller. Video- and audiotapes are available through libraries, book stores, and the Buckminster Fuller Institute (see appendix C).
16. See Fuller, *Critical Path* (as per chapter 1 note 40), p. 125.
17. See Fuller and Applewhite, *Synergetics* (as per chapter 1 note 45); Fuller and Applewhite, *Synergetics 2* (as per chapter 2 note 111); and Edmondson (as per chapter 2 note 31).
18. See chapter 1 note 41.
19. Precession is defined and explained on pages 55-58. See also Fuller, *Critical Path* (as per chapter 1 note 40).
20. Dymaxion is defined on page 61; see also chapter 2 note 59.
21. See Fuller, *Critical Path;* and Fuller and Applewhite, *Synergetics* (as per chapter 1 note 45), section 700.00. See also Ingber (as per chapter 2 note 30).
22. The first eight of these categories are paraphrased from William F. O'Neill, *Educational Ideologies: Contemporary Expressions of Educational Philosophy* (Santa Monica, California: Goodyear Publishing Co., 1981), p. 109. See also Gerber (as per chapter 2 note 135).
23. See chapter 2 note 146.

Appendix B

1. See appendix A note 14.
2. See chapter 3 note 51.
3. See appendix A note 3.

Appendix D

1. Getting started with a drumming circle/percussion group using small, hand-held instruments is easy: The group can establish a steady beat by playing what many consider the ultimate rhythm and also the simplest, a slow, deliberate, and steady 1 1 1, etc., with moderate pauses between each beat. This pattern is often used in healing journeys and meditations. Another basic rhythm is the heartbeat.

Some might want to experiment by playing the "and" or the "and uh" that exists between the beats (1 and 2 and, etc., or 1 and uh 2 and uh, etc.), perhaps playing only on certain "ands," "and uhs," or "uhs," using a triangle or shaker. Rests can be inserted to add yet another dimension. The rests are as vital as the played beats; it can be less interesting when there is no "space" in the music. Cycles (measures) consisting of odd or even numbers of beats can be created, for example, with hand claps in slow 7s: clap rest clap rest clap clap rest (and perhaps a gradual introduction of other instruments into the mix). Some participants can begin to play this rhythm in double time, while holding to the pattern or cyclically varying it here and there, creating compelling effects. Drumming does not have to be an intellectual counting exercise—just feel the pulse.

An infinitude of variations and nuances becomes possible when the distinct tones produced by each percussion instrument are added along with accentuated beats, rests, tempo changes, and dynamic variations (even vocalizations), and when rhythms are discovered within rhythms. Since ancient times it has been known that drumming is healing. During group percussion, when everyone listens to the whole, the experience can be magical.

"Drumming promotes healing by creating wholeness between parts of ourselves," notes the frame drummer and recording artist Glen Velez (*The Glen Velez Website: The World of Frame Drums,* 2000, "Glen Velez: An Interview with Iris Brooks," 17 July 2000 <www.glenvelez.com/ibchakra.html>). Another source of information for creating informal hand-held percussion interactions (in families, schools, etc., even for very young children) is Jamtown. When passing around instruments for a percussion jam session, its founder, John Hayden, tells each person to "play a beat you can repeat" (*The Road to Jamtown: A Percussion Activities Guide* [1995; rpt. Seattle: Jamtown, LLC, 1997], p. 3; see also <www.jamtown.com>).

In creating informal hand-held percussion/drumming circles, it is important to remember that the beauty and fun lie in the simplicity and not so much in learned technique.

Epigraph

The Zen Teaching of Huang Po (as per chapter 3 note 7), p. 103.

Mind is a mighty ocean, a sea which knows no bounds.
Words are but scarlet lotus to cure the lesser ills.

HUANG PO

Alex Gerber Jr. (Ph.D., theoretical foundations of education, University of Southern California) is an educator, counselor, and musician. His company, Gerber Educational Resources, is dedicated to the advancement of holistic awareness and the implementation of holistic solutions. To order publications, call 800-247-6553 (outside the USA and Canada call 419-281-1802) or visit www.wholenessbook.com.